THAT GUY'S WEARING RED TOO!

Exploring the State of Nebraska and its unique
football tradition

Steve Banner

Banner Business Services

Fort Worth, TX

Steve Banner/Banner Business Services
Fort Worth, TX
www.nebraskacollegefootball.com

Cover design by Holly Sosa.

Book Layout © 2014 BookDesignTemplates.com

That Guy's Wearing Red Too!/ Steve Banner. -- 1st ed.
ISBN 978-0986434136

For Tom Hauser, the first guy I ever saw dressed in Husker red.

"Courage; Generosity; Fairness; Honor; In these are the true awards of manly sport."
HARTLEY BURR ALEXANDER
(Words from the former UNL professor of philosophy inscribed on the northwest side of Memorial Stadium)

CONTENTS

TWO GUYS IN RED

"That guy was wearing red, too!" I breathlessly informed Tom. It was the Labor Day weekend in 2002 and I was making my second-ever visit to Nebraska. My wife and I had arrived in Omaha late on Friday evening to spend 3 nights with her parents at their home across the street from the Ak-Sar-Ben horse race track. We had brought our large dog with us and of course she needed her exercise, so I arose early on Saturday morning to take her out for a walk. But just as I was about to leave the house, my father-in-law Tom emerged from his bedroom wearing a red Nebraska t-shirt.

When I asked him about it he informed that today would be the Opening Day of the college football season and that it was his personal tradition to always wear a red shirt on a game day. I complimented him on his team spirit and set off with the dog for a 15-minute stroll around the quiet and leafy neighborhood. There was very little traffic on the road since it was so early in the day, but I did notice one particular car that drove past in which the driver was wearing red. I couldn't wait to get back to tell Tom that I had seen someone else who seemed to share his same tradition of wearing red on a game day. "That guy was wearing red, too!" I blurted out with enthusiastically, thinking that I had found probably the only other person in Nebraska besides Tom who was wearing a red shirt that day.

I was soon to learn that the tradition of wearing red on a game day in Nebraska extends vastly beyond Tom and his Omaha neighbor. My initiation to the world of Nebraska and the Big Red had begun. And the more I learned, the more intrigued I became.

I have been lucky enough to have lived in a number of different countries and cultures around the world while experiencing major sporting events such as ice hockey in Stockholm and Montreal, NFL football in Miami and Dallas, and even camel races in Saudi Arabia. However I have seen something unique in the way that Nebraskans are proud of both their 37th State in the Union and the college football team that bears its name.

I was first exposed to Nebraska football by my wife's parents, who were season ticket holders and alumni of the school, having met and married in Lincoln. Over the subsequent 14 years since my first trip to Nebraska I had become more and more intrigued by the way the entire state seemed to unite around their beloved Big Red, and hence my desire to write a book about the people and the team to which they seem to feel such a sense of belonging.

My plan was to attend every home game during the 2015 season, spending the Thursday and Friday leading up to each game in a different Nebraska town where I would meet with local residents and explore their links to history and the Big Red football program. After each game I would attend the post-game news conference for further insights from the coaches and players on the events of the day. On each of the weeks that the team played away from home I would visit a Husker Fan Club in a different part of the country. I also tried to make plans to interview prominent fans along the way such as Larry the Cable Guy and Warren Buffet.

As a result of executing this plan, each chapter of this book represents a single week of the Huskers' 2015 season. Although I was ultimately unsuccessful in my attempts to make contact with the above-mentioned celebrity fans, the book is a description of my physical and personal journey as I witnessed and recorded what turned out to be a topsy-turvy season all the way from Opening Day to Bowl Day.

I only hope that you enjoy reading about my adventures as much as I enjoyed the journey and the generous-of-spirit Nebraskans that I met along the way!

CHAPTER ONE

OMAHA IS JUST EXPLODING

Despite my father-in-law Tom informing my wife and I every time we visited the largest city in Nebraska that it was thriving and expanding at such a rapid pace that it was "exploding", I was gratified to see while crossing the Missouri River into Omaha that the city had not yet disintegrated into a pile of rubble after growing so fast that it simply collapsed under its own weight.

Although Omaha may have had a population of more than 400,000 people at the time of the passing of my father-in-law in 2010, I would wager that there were very few of his fellow residents who were more proud of the city than Tom Hauser. Every time my wife and I visited from Texas, Tom would be happy to greet us with the latest news about new developments in his beloved home town. "Omaha is just exploding!" was a phrase he often used.

Although Tom was initially dubious about the new baseball field being built to house the College World Series, by the time the stadium and its surrounding improvements were finished he was very pleased with the results. He was proud to tell us about other local highlights such as Omaha's "world-class zoo", the Lauritzen Gardens, the redeveloped parks along the Missouri River and the airport that he felt was designed just about perfectly. He always enjoyed showing us around the city and nearby attractions during our visits, and we enjoyed hearing his colorful recollections as we drove past various iconic locations such as Gorat's steakhouse restaurant.

My wife and I would listen obligingly to Tom's enthusiastic descriptions, but we both felt he had gone too far the day that he took us by the character-filled building that used to be the Blackstone Hotel. "Here", he announced with evident pride, "is where the Reuben sandwich was invented." My wife and I just looked at one another as we were both thinking that everyone knows the Reuben sandwich was invented in New York. We both felt a little bit sorry for him and hoped he hadn't told too many other visitors that same misguided story. Nevertheless the image of the Blackstone was etched in our minds together with a fond memory of a man who was very happy to remain exactly where he was, as opposed to those restless souls who spend their whole lives searching for the "right" place to live.

Although I had visited Omaha on numerous occasions, given that the Omaha-centric Tom was my tour guide I had never crossed the Missouri and set foot in Iowa. As a result, my entry into Omaha from the direction of Iowa on the Thursday evening before Labor Day was a new experience. It was also somewhat exciting in an unforeseen way as I drove towards the setting sun that made it almost impossible to read the signs above the highway that I was relying on to find my way to my hotel on the west side of downtown.

Fortunately the traffic at 7.30 on a Thursday evening was not busy and thus several times I was able to change lanes abruptly after realizing I was headed for the wrong exit from the highway. But I eventually found my way to the hotel after silently thanking the traffic gods that my wife had been born in Omaha and not New York.

Perhaps my level of concentration on my driving had not been as intense as it should have been, given that for the previous hour as I drove across Iowa I had been listening to a radio show previewing the Nebraska football season that was to get underway in "less than 48 hours!", as several excited callers to the radio station noted with eager anticipation. The new Head Coach Mike Riley was a guest in the studio and he received a warm welcome from both the hosts of the show and the fans who called in – one of whom noted that he had been ready for the new season to begin ever since the Red/White Spring Scrimmage game in April.

To the uninitiated, a statement such as this might seem a bit far-fetched. After all, the scrimmage game was only intended for the purpose of practice and it had taken place some five months earlier. Who could possibly get excited about a practice game smack in the middle of the off-season? But let's not forget that this is Nebraska football we're talking about, where 76,881 fans in the stadium and a national audience on the Big Ten Network tuned in to watch the players and coaches run through their paces. Unfortunately I had been out of the country and unable to attend or see the game for myself, but I have no doubt that there were plenty of people present who were just as excited as that particular caller to the radio show.

Judging by his performance on the show, I received a very good impression of Coach Riley. He sounded very genuine and approachable as he capably answered the questions posed to him. Particularly impressive was his answer to the question of how he would measure his success in his first season at Nebraska. To paraphrase his response, he said that he was trying to "instill a set of values" into the players, and his level of success in this endeavor would be one of his success measurement criteria along with the number of games the team won. Given that he was about to start his first season as head coach of a team whose fan base is accustomed to a high level of success on the field, for him to talk about helping his charges to become members of society as well as better football players was not only refreshing to hear but also courageous on his part. After all, the previous coach had been fired after winning 9 games in his final year.

During a discussion about the players who had been recruited and would fall under Riley's wing, one of the hosts told a story about a recruiting technique used by Nebraska during its glory days to help persuade prospects who were not quite sure whether to sign up with the Big Red. Sitting in the family living room with the potential player and his parents, the recruiter would summarize the situations as follows: "Well son, the way I see it you have two choices. You can either come to Nebraska and win games, or you can go to another school and get beaten by Nebraska."

When the discussion turned to the coming game two days away, Riley did not skirt around the question asked by a caller about how he viewed the various components of the BYU team. He responded in very frank fashion, comparing the Nebraska offense, defense and special teams against the BYU opponents they would soon face. In summary his analysis was that Nebraska would have to work very hard to keep up with BYU but he had faith that his team was prepared for the task.

Neither did he sidestep the matter of five Nebraska players who had been suspended for the first game as a result of their violation of team rules some three weeks earlier. The identities of the players had previously been kept hidden but their names had been made public during the prior couple of days. This to me seemed like a sensible approach to the matter- the players' names were kept quiet for a few weeks to avoid the distraction of a media frenzy, and now they were released just before they served their suspensions.

This was in contrast to the approach BYU took to the four players that they would suspend for the same game. The BYU names had been initially kept hidden and were not released until just before the game. While I can understand that a coach may not want to give his opposing counterpart the advantage of knowing in advance which players would not be in the line-up, I applaud the action of Nebraska to release the names of their players far enough in advance so that the public can see who they are and not overlook them in all the excitement of the game. In addition to building a football team, Coach Riley clearly wants to build men who take responsibility for their actions.

But enough about football. It was almost 8 o'clock as I left the hotel on foot after checking in and I had not yet had dinner. I had seen a Runza's a few blocks away from the hotel and was anxious to try this Nebraskan delight that I had not yet had the occasion to sample, despite having heard so much about it. As I walked through the streets I heard the sound of an open-air concert taking place close by in one of the lovely outdoor spaces that had been pointed out by Tom during our previous visits as evidence of the ongoing explosion of the city. I paused for a few minutes to take in the warm evening scene with families seated on deck chairs or on the grass, not realizing that this short delay in my progress was to have unintended consequences.

It was 8.04pm by the time I arrived at Runza's, where I found to my considerable dismay that the doors were locked for the night. The sign on the door informed me that counter service hours finish at 8pm – precisely, apparently - although drive-through service continues for several more hours. While I have learned to mimic the voices and mannerisms of certain classmates and politicians over the years – and the occasional bird call – I did not trust my ability to pretend to be a car, not even a hybrid model, and thus I had no choice but to look elsewhere for my evening sustenance.

Why a popular fast-food restaurant would choose to close its doors at 8pm on a warm evening with hundreds of pedestrians in the immediate vicinity is beyond me. Perhaps it's because the taste of the house specialty is so irresistible that the only defense against the hordes of late-night customers who descend upon the establishment in salivating swarms is to close the doors at 8pm before the stampede becomes too hard to manage? Maybe that's why they call it "fast food" – you have to get their fast before they lock the doors. No matter the reason, I would have to wait until another day to be initiated into the mysterious would of Runza's.

As I walked along the street I noticed several other restaurants nearby, all of which were securely locked against the scourge of any late-night (i.e. post-8pm) patrons who may dare to try to order dinner at such an ungodly hour. Eventually I happened upon a Mexican restaurant with an Italian name that still had its lights on, even though the large dining room appeared to be entirely empty. Fortunately the establishment was still open and I joined the two fashionably-late-dining couples who remained, and ordered what turned out to be quite a delicious pizza. I enjoyed a beer with my meal and would have liked to order a glass of wine, except that the waitress kept avoiding me lest I keep her too late by lingering over my glass. As soon as I left the restaurant together with the last of the two late-dining couples, I realized why everyone seemed to be in such a hurry to close up and leave town.

I heard the first explosion as soon as I set foot on the street, and saw the accompanying flash. Tom had been right all along – Omaha was indeed exploding!

I walked cautiously toward the sound as the explosions continued and flashes of colored light lit up the sky. Hundreds of people sat pinned to their deck chairs or on their blankets by the ongoing detonations, staring at the sky and afraid to move a muscle. The stylish buildings surrounding the park were illuminated over and over by flashes of color as the spectacular barrage continued for a full 15 minutes. I too was transfixed by the display of sight and sound until eventually the final explosions were followed by loud cheers and applause from the crowd. The poor unsuspecting souls had thought it all had been an elaborate fireworks display in anticipation of Labor Day, but thanks to Tom I knew better. I just hoped no-one in the crowd was hungry and planning to have a quick dinner before going home.

Later that evening my wife flew in from Fort Worth, and as we drove back towards the city along Abbott Drive we admired the ambiance of the pretty boulevard with its trees and light fixtures that we felt created a pleasant and welcoming feeling for visitors to the city. I didn't have the heart to break the peaceful mood by telling my wife about the loud incendiary events that had taken place a few hours earlier.

The next morning saw the front page of the Omaha World-Herald occupied almost entirely with football pictures and news, while also asking the question whether its readers were ready for game day. At the very bottom of the page was the beginning of an article concerning the Omaha waterfront and how to make the most of the beauty offered by the Missouri River right on the edge of the city. Thanks to our ever-enthusiastic personal tour guide, my wife and I had indeed witnessed the evolution of the development that had taken place in the area during the last 14 years.

The pedestrian footbridge named after Bob Kerrey was a particular favorite of ours and we had often admired the way in which it was illuminated at night and created a glowing link across the sky between the two shores. However I could not help but chuckle when I read the less-than-glowing assessment made by Tom Murphy, the former mayor of Pittsburgh. Although saying that the bridge is one of the best he has seen, he also noted that "It's a bridge that goes from nowhere, to nowhere." I immediately thought of another chap named Tom who would have offered a rather different point of view.

After our quick review of the paper we headed over to meet long-time friends of my wife's parents for breakfast at a diner near the Aksarben Village development.

At the time of my first visit to Omaha, this area was home to a horse racing track as well as an ice rink where my father-in-law had played hockey in his younger days. We had witnessed the transformation of the area over the years into a residential and shopping area, and were also pleased to see that a new ice rink was in the final stages of construction. Pat and Judd live in one of the condo buildings facing the afore-mentioned pedestrian bridge and although I was curious, I felt it to be too early in the day to ask their opinion of Mr. Mur-phy's views of the structure they see every day through their living room window. Steering clear of a serious discussion turned out to be a wise decision as it seemed the waitress was almost incapable of maintaining our caffeine levels by refill-ing our coffee cups. I had originally asked for a cup of decaf, which eventually arrived after a long delay. I finally decided not to complicate things by asking for a refill of decaf and decided instead that regular coffee would be better than noth-ing. And nothing was what I got. I did not make a fuss but figured the waitress must have still been in shell shock after the explosive events of the previous night that had taken place just a few miles away.

After caffeine-deprived but otherwise enjoyable breakfast, my wife and I spent most of the day driving around Omaha and visiting various locations including the building that used to house the Blackstone Hotel. Although the building is now used as a company headquarters office, it has been lovingly maintained and still bears the Blackstone name on its awning. After we had finished admiring the building and chuckling about the Reuben sandwich in-vention claim which by now had become part of family folklore, my

wife decided to use her phone to google the matter and settle the origins of the sandwich once and for all. Was it invented in New York or perhaps New Jersey? This was the sum extent of any mystery that remained in our minds about the whole matter.

Thanks to the magic of the internet we soon got to the meat of the matter, so to speak. It seems that the Reuben sandwich was indeed invented at the Blackstone Hotel by a certain Lithuanian-born grocer named Reuben Kulakofsky who lived in Omaha. Apparently he was a member of a group who played poker at the hotel each week from 1920 to 1935. The poker group also included the hotel's owner who liked the sandwich so much that he put it on the lunchtime menu. The rest, as they say, is history. Tom had been right all along and we had been wrong to doubt him. Our faces turned as red as corned beef along with our feelings of guilt.

If we had disappointed Tom by not believing his Reuben sandwich story, he would have practically disowned me as a son-in-law if he had known that I had driven to Nebraska to watch his beloved Big Red but had forgotten to bring my red shirt with me. Although there seemed to be no shortage of places in Omaha where I could buy Nebraska clothing or accessories, my wife recommended Husker Hounds as *the* place to go. After our arrival I soon found that she was not exaggerating when she told me that I could find every conceivable Nebraska item in the Husker Hounds store.

Apart from the usual shirts and caps that I expected to find, they had socks, shoelaces, underwear, pajamas, bandanas, clothes pins, cups, Christmas ornaments and the list goes on. My wife recalls that they also used to stock toilet paper but I wasn't brave enough to ask the store clerk if and where it might be found. However we did find a small bandana and collar that would fit our little 12-pound husker hound at home. I was able to buy a nice polo shirt for myself, but my wife declined my offer to pay for the on-site cosmetic technician to decorate her nails with the team colors and logo.

That evening we dined at another Omaha institution and a place frequented by my father-in-law: Gorat's Steak House. Tom lived nearby and would dine at Gorat's every Friday, where his favorite waitress Rita would show him to his regular table upon which she had already placed a glass of the red wine he liked to order. The restaurant was founded in 1944 and has served many famous people their "finest steaks in the world" as the advertising sign in front of the building promises. Warren Buffett has been a long-time customer who continues to eat there regularly according to all reports.

Saturday morning dawned clear and sunny with a predicted game-time temperature of 93 degrees, which would equal a long-standing record if the prediction turned out to be correct. Fans planning to attend the game were informed through the media that they could bring two bottles of water into the stadium with them, and this was a message that was only too well understood by all concerned as we shall see later.

Upon our arrival in Lincoln we noticed that it, too had undergone a number of changes since our last visit in 2009 although as far as we knew it was not in any imminent danger of exploding. The first thing we noticed was that a number of new parking garages had been constructed, each of which was advertising a price that we hoped was expressed in Italian Lira. We both vaguely recalled Tom taking us to an open dirt area near a train line that was used for parking at the rate of $10, however we soon found that both the open area and its

$10 price tag were long gone. We finally worked our way through the heavy traffic to come back to a double-story parking garage where we tried our best to speak Italian, only to be informed by the attendant that the number on the sign was in fact US dollars, cash only.

But the whole ordeal of searching for parking had made us work up an appetite for lunch, and thus we quickly adjourned to the nearest watering hole. As if by predestination, one of the items featured prominently on the menu was the Reuben Sandwich. We both felt we owed Tom an apology for having doubted him and we offered atonement for our sins by enjoying a satisfying repast of a Reuben Sandwich accompanied by a red beer, which had been a favorite of Tom's on a game day.

That whole red beer on game day is a very practical idea when you stop to think about it: it doesn't matter if you happen to spill some of the drink on yourself, because you're guaranteed to be wearing a red shirt at the time.

The first item of business after lunch was to buy tickets for the game, which was something I planned to do on the street rather than trying to buy them on line in advance. My reasoning was that by buying tickets this way I was likely to encounter some interesting characters and experiences that I could include in my account of the season. As it turned out, I didn't have to wait long and I was not disappointed with the results.

Not far from where we had parked, we encountered a man who was both buying and selling tickets. I had previously met people outside stadiums in other cities who were selling tickets, and I had met people who wanted to buy tickets for themselves. However I had never met anyone who was both buying and selling at the same time. At first glance I thought it would make an interesting case study for a business school program to witness not only the setting or prices and margins for each ticket but also the psychology of the sale and the negotiation that goes along with it. In any case I approached the man, whose name turned out to be Bob, and asked if he had two tickets.

His immediate response upon hearing my accent was to ask where I was from. When I told him I was Australian, he initiated a well-informed discussion about the refugee situation in Australia and Europe that was making headlines at the time. He then went on to tell me who his favorite Australian singer was – I thought he would say Olivia Newton-John or Rick Springfield or perhaps Keith Urban – but he astounded me when he said Joan Sutherland (a famous coloratura soprano opera singer who passed away in 2010 and was once called by Luciano Pavarotti the "Voice of the Century"). After a brief discussion of her storied career we walked away with two tickets in our hands and my head spinning at the thought of a street ticket-seller versed in both current affairs and international opera.

Our seats were high up in the south end zone, almost directly behind the goal. This gave us a good view of the whole field as well as the scoreboard screen at the north end. We squeezed into our seats in the 93 degree heat and watched the pre-game activities. However as soon as the game started, everyone in the crowd stood up. I hoped that this was not a new tradition that had begun since our last visit five years ago and that people would not stand for the entire game. Our friend Pat had warned us that morning that one of the reasons she no longer goes to watch the game was because many people stand rather than sit to watch the action. I am over 6 feet tall, so standing up does not impair my own view but I feel sorry for those behind me who are shorter, not to mention those who are older and don't have the stamina to stand up for three hours in a crowded stadium.

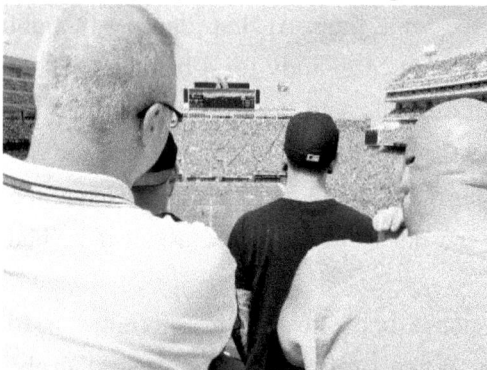

Just as predicted by the forecasters, the conditions were sunny and hot which must have been hard for the players to endure. The fans were certainly suffering, and the newspapers reported the next day that some 130 fans were treated by the Red Cross for heat-related problems by the time the game was half over. Many fans had either brought plastic bottles of water with them or purchased them on site and it seemed there was a steady flow of empty bottles appearing under our feet in the stands, steadily flowing downhill as we pushed them forward with our feet just as the fans behind us had done. I pitied the poor patrons in the bottom couple of rows in the stands whom I visualized would be buried up to their waists in empty plastic bottles by the time the game ended.

Nebraska was first to score, halfway through the first quarter with a 14-yard touchdown pass to Westerkamp who avoided several defenders as he ran to the end zone. As the red balloons drifted skyward in celebration and the band played the fight song, the fans around us began to take their seats as if they could relax now that the first score was on the board. We too were much relieved about the turn of events and sat down in our allocated 18 inches of bench space to watch the game.

Coach Riley had talked about BYU's tall receivers during his pregame review on the radio a couple of nights earlier, and it didn't take long before the BYU quarterback put his tall targets to use. Nebraska's defensive line was not putting much pressure on the BYU quarterback and by the end of the first half the visitors had created a 24-14 lead for themselves and they looked like running away with the game.

However thanks to some half-time adjustments, the Black-shirts began to assert themselves in style during the third quarter. Of the four BYU possessions during the quarter, one of them ended with an interception by Nate Gerry, another ended with a turnover on downs and the other two were three-and-out. Meanwhile the Huskers scored two touchdowns to take the lead and bring the score to 28-24 to end the quarter.

By halfway through the fourth quarter, BYU had scored a field goal to bring them within one point of tying the Huskers. By the time Nebraska's final drive began with just over four minutes left in the game, the Huskers had already stalled on two drives in the quarter after failing to convert third and one opportunities. BYU had also punted twice during the quarter after going three-and-out on both occasions.

But on this final drive the Huskers looked solid as they used 6 plays to move the ball 46 yards to the BYU 22-yard line. However on third and three they lost two yards and had to settle for the field goal attempt from the BYU 24-yard line. Unfortunately the kicker missed his attempt – his second miss for the day - and BYU regained possession 76 yards from the Nebraska end zone with 48 seconds left on the clock. At this stage the odds favored the home team – not only because of the large distance and short amount of time available – but also because BYU's starting quarterback had been injured earlier in the quarter and his backup was now tasked with the difficult challenge of driving the team down the field to score.

The score was 28-27 in favor of Nebraska as the back-up BYU quarterback during the course of six plays moved the ball to Nebraska's 42-yard line. But there was only 1 second left in the game and the ball was too far away to attempt a field goal. BYU would have to run one final play to try to score a touchdown against heavy odds. I could see clearly from my vantage point that three of Nebraska's Blackshirts were lined up in the south end zone waiting for the start of the final play of the game as the crowd of 89,959 held its collective breath. And then.....Nebraska called a time-out.

As the players and coaches huddled, my mind wandered to the 12 penalties for 90 yards that the home team had gifted the visitors and the two missed field goals that would have made such a difference on the scoreboard. But I was soon brought back to the present moment by the roar of the crowd as the players lined up again for the final play.

The ball was snapped, the BYU quarterback dropped back and eventually ran to his right while ignoring the potential receivers who criss-crossed in front of him 20 yards from the well-defended end zone. Eventually succumbing to the relentless pressure from the Nebraska pass rushers, he threw a wobbly Hail Mary pass towards the end zone that seemed to be directed at no-one in particular. In my mind the game was over and Nebraska had won. But somehow, inexplicably, the ball landed in the arms of a white BYU jersey and that jersey held on to the ball as it landed just over the goal line into the end zone. The deafening roar of the red-clad crowd was stunned into silence and replaced by the joyous celebrations of the BYU fans who had been grouped into three small islands of blue among the vast sea of red. I had witnessed a moment that will long be remembered by Nebraska fans young and old, standing or sitting.

The final score: BYU 33 Nebraska 28.

If the result had been reversed, Mike Riley would have been the sixth consecutive Husker head coach to win his debut game, dating back to Bob Devaney in 1962. A win would have also been the team's 30th consecutive home opener victory, the longest in the nation. But records are made to be broken and I looked forward to the next game against South Alabama where Riley would have the opportunity to record his first win for Nebraska.

CHAPTER TWO

PERFECT DAYS IN KEARNEY

I must admit to having a very favorable predisposition to Kearney and its people long before I visited the town for the first time during the days leading up to the Huskers' second game of the season. The reason for my prejudice towards Kearney was due to my friend Vinay who had moved there from Dallas some five years ago to take up a job in his chosen field of Industrial Engineering. While there is usually nothing remarkable about someone relocating to another American state with their employment, Vinay's case was different than most and it added to my already positive views about Nebraska and its people.

Vinay was born and raised in India, then came to the U.S. to further his college education. Like the millions of other young people from overseas who have come to this country on a Student Visa, he hoped that an education in America would give him access to new horizons of opportunity. He hoped that after completing his education he may be able to find productive employment in the U.S. and perhaps be able to obtain citizenship in due course. Vinay was certainly not alone with his ambitions, as large numbers of his fellow visiting students have the same aim but only a few succeed in reaching this goal.

Without wading into the debate about immigration that raises its head on a regular basis in the world of American politics, it should be noted that a legal mechanism does exist in the system for foreign students to be able to stay and work in the U.S. after completing their education. However path toward this goal is both complex and expensive for all concerned. The window of opportunity for the students opens when they complete the degree program for which their visa was granted. From that point onwards the students have 12 months in which they legally can live and work in the country before they must leave. Some students use this period for the purpose of vacation or sight-seeing before returning home, while many others use it to try and find a job which will allow them to stay longer in the U.S.

But the major complication that arises for students such as Vinay who seek to stay and work in the U.S. is that not only must they be able to find an employer willing to hire them, but that employer must also be willing to sponsor a new temporary visa for the foreign-born employee. Visas of this type are not only expensive for the employer and limited in number, but these visas will not be granted unless the employer is able to demonstrate that the job vacancy in question has been extensively advertised and no suitable American candidate could be found.

Vinay applied for numerous jobs all over the country during his yearlong waiting period with no success. Meanwhile he worked in a variety of part-time positions in the Dallas area to make ends meet and pay his rent. Vinay must have become increasingly concerned as the months ticked by with no good news on the job front, but he maintained an outwardly cheery disposition despite the unsettling uncertainty of his immediate future. And then one day just a few weeks away from his departure deadline he received the good news from Nebraska, that a filter manufacturer was willing to take him on as an employee.

While all of his friends in Dallas were sad at the thought of losing his smiling face from among our ranks, we were thrilled for him that his hard work and persistence had paid off (and just in time!). We knew Vinay as a very bright young man and a hard worker, and were very happy that his employer-to-be had recognized the same characteristics in him and was willing to give him the opportunity to prove himself. To me, this whole episode seemed to reflect a wonderful Nebraska spirit: if you're willing to move here and work hard, we'll be glad to welcome you into our community. I could imagine this was a philosophy my wife's great-great-grandparents encountered when they homesteaded in Nebraska during the second half of the 19th Century.

Speaking for myself I was not disappointed with the Nebraska welcome I received upon my arrival in Kearney, beginning with the moment Vinay and I went to dinner at a restaurant in Kearney shortly after I had checked in to my hotel. The very first people we encountered were a smiling couple who were just leaving the restaurant but stopped and held the door open for us to enter. It reminded me of a partly-in-jest quote that I used to hear when I lived in Stockholm during the 1990s among the very private and often emotionally-distant Swedes:

"When a complete stranger smiles at you and says hello, it means he is either insane or American".

On the other hand, Kearney represents the complete opposite of the above approach to life. In Kearney, and I daresay in
Nebraska in general, a person that the Swedes would call a
"stranger" is simply regarded as someone that you have not
yet met.

During the next forty-eight hours I was able to meet and
talk with a number of people who live and work in Kearney
and who each embodied a sense of friendliness and warmth.
More importantly they projected a feeling of contentment with
life in Kearney and its surrounds – a sense that individuals
and families had found the right location to make their home.

For example on Friday morning I met with Woody at the
colorfully-named and colorfully-decorated "Chug a Lug

Sports Bar" on the east side
of town. He had been raised
in a town nearby before joining the Navy and serving
during the Vietnam era in
Japan and the Far East. After
his six-year period of service
was over, rather than re-
enlist and see more of the
world he informed his supe-
riors that he wanted to return
to Kearney because he felt it to be a great place to raise a family.

Woody has been a Huskers season ticket holder since
1993, having driven 130 miles in each direction to and from
games in Lincoln for more than twenty years. He recalls his
favorite memory of the team as being from 1994 when Nebraska beat Colorado 24-7 in front of 76,000 fans in Lincoln.

He remembers walking towards the stadium an hour before kickoff and hearing the roar of the crowd which was already getting excited for the game. As a comparatively recent convert to Big Red football, I had been unaware of the history of rivalry between the two teams but Woody recounted a story from that day in 1993 to illustrate the point.

Since he was early to the game, he stood for a little while outside the stadium where he witnessed the following exchange between a ticket seller in the street and a Colorado fan dressed in team colors.

"Have you got any tickets?"

"Yeah, but I've only got one left. Its $300."

"$300! That's way too much. You're just setting that price because I'm a Colorado fan!"

"Nope, it's $300. Take it or leave it."

The Colorado fan walked away without buying, muttering to himself with his head hung low in dejection. Then a Nebraska fan in a red shirt approached the ticket seller.

"Have you got any tickets?"

"Yeah, but I've only got one left. Its $100".

The Fall season is Woody's favorite time of year since it represents the harvest being completed, the opening of hunting seasons for pheasant and deer, pleasant weather and of course Big Red football. Summarizing his Fall contentment with a line of poetry he quoted: "Then, if ever, come perfect days." Just as had been the case for my father-in-law Tom, I could see that Woody had found his ideal place to live and he loved everything about it.

The articulate Woody also summarized his view of the principles that should guide Nebraska fans: "You represent the State of Nebraska when you're at a game", and in response to games such as last week's heart-breaking loss to BYU: "If you can't lose with class, it diminishes both you and your program." I thought these were very wise words, and they coincided with the inscription above each entrance to Memorial Stadium: "Through these gates pass the greatest fans in college football".

However this simple affirmation regarding those who pass through the gates can mean different things to different people. To people such as Woody and myself it means that Nebraska fans are courteous and well-behaved, generous in their praise of both their own team and their opponents, and respectful of the decisions made by the referees.

To some other people the definition of a "great" fan stretches in a different direction in which one's level of passion for one's own team is demonstrated through actions of another kind. This includes acts such as booing the opposing team and the referees, and getting into fights with fans of the opposing team. In recent years we have seen this attitude taken to extremes in some other sports where the fans celebrate the winning of a championship by rioting in the streets and burning overturned police cars.

We may never know for certain exactly which sentiments the author of the inscription above the gates was trying to encapsulate, but for a final word on the matter let's turn to another Big Red football tradition.

The following is the Husker Prayer that the players say before a game just prior to walking through the tunnel on to the field:

"Dear Lord,
In the battles we go through life
We ask for a chance that's fair
A chance to equal all our strife
A chance to do or dare
And if we win
Let it be by the code
With faith and honor held high
And if we lose,
Let us stand by the road
And cheer as the winners go by.
Day by day
We get better and better
A team that can't be beat
Won't be beat."

In my view we now have a clear answer to the question of what constitutes a "great" Nebraska fan. It's someone who follows in the stands the same code of conduct that the players are expected to follow on the field.

That same evening I had the opportunity to meet a number of employees of one of the largest companies in Kearney, who had gathered to say farewell to my friend Vinay as he prepared to change jobs and move to Seattle after 5 years in the warm embrace of Kearney. Several of the older gentlemen reported relocating to the area some 30 years ago and finding the streets and stores eerily deserted during a Huskers game.

Kevin had relocated from Michigan and he recalled walking through a mall in the nearby larger town of Grand Island and hearing the radio broadcast of the game over the mall's PA system (presumably to compensate those poor souls who due to some urgent situation at home had no choice but to make a hurried trip to the mall while the game was on).

Kevin's wife remembers a time when she went to a department store to get him some new trousers, but she was not sure he would like the pair she had picked out. The problem was easily solved by the store clerk who told her to take the trousers home to show her husband. If he liked them, she could return next week to pay. But if he didn't like them she could simply bring them back to the store.

Then there was another friend of hers had bought a loveseat sofa from a store and couldn't wait to get it home. Unfortunately the store's only delivery truck was miles away and would not be able to deliver the sofa until the next day. In this case the problem was quickly solved by the store manager who put the sofa on top of the back seat of his new Cadillac convertible and delivered it to the delighted customer's home that same day.

It was everyday incidents like these that endeared Kearney and its people to the transplanted Michiganders and many others. Even after only two days arrived in this charming town of 31,000 people, I could see why they liked it and I hope to be able to return.

Unlike the couple from Michigan, Jesse and his wife had grown up in another town some 50 miles from Kearney where they were accustomed to watching the Huskers game in a local bar. This particular establishment had a tradition of its own, in which a large drinking vessel made out of a cow's hoof was kept behind the bar until game day. Prior to the start of the game the hoof glass was filled with a combination of exotic liquors that changed from one week to the next, and every time Nebraska scored a touchdown the drinking vessel was passed among all of the patrons in celebration. Over the course of time this custom became so much a part of the couple's own tradition that they borrowed the hoof glass and passed it around among the guests at their wedding.

The game against South Alabama was to start at 7pm, which gave the tailgaters ample time to enjoy the fine afternoon before the kickoff. The previous week I had witnessed the sight of several fans dressed in red as Elvis in one of the tailgate areas and I was determined to meet up with them to see which one of their number was actually the *real* Elvis. I thought it was quite a stroke of genius for Elvis to hide in plain sight after faking his death all those years ago. With all those decoys around him he would have plenty of time to escape if any IRS Revenue Agents or ex-wives came snooping around. However I ran out of time before the game and had to postpone my quest to find The King until another day.

I had been delayed in part because Opera Bob had run out of tickets by the time I arrived. But rather than let me find my own way, Bob walked with me towards the stadium until he found a fan with an extra ticket to sell. He then negotiated with the fan on my behalf and bought the ticket. Where else but Nebraska would you find a street ticket seller who would go out of his way like that for someone he'd only met once? I tipped him $5 for his trouble but it felt like I should have given him more.

I thought afterwards about the lady buying trousers for her husband in Kearney – could I not have simply taken the ticket from the fan and then paid him later on the condition that I liked the game? If Nebraska lost, or I had too many fans around me standing, I'd just give his ticket back to him after the game.

Before walking up to my seat I decided to learn a lesson from the previous week and rent a stadium seat, which consists of a steel-framed seat with a cushion and backrest that sits on top of the normal plank seating. I found that not only did this seat provide much-appreciated cushioning and support in key areas, it also served to define my allocated seat space and prevent the encroaching that normally happens throughout the course of a game. The only disadvantage was that my knees were now much closer to the back of the person in front of me, but the particular young man affected in this case seemed to take it all in good stride.

Nebraska played a much-improved game compared to last week's narrow loss against BYU and ended up winning 48-9 over a game South Alabama team that never stopped trying. At the press conference after the game Coach Mike Riley entered the room with a smile that displayed the sense of relief he was obviously feeling after his first win for Nebraska. Although, as he said, it was "a week late" he was clearly happy that not only had his team won but they had done so while correcting a number of the facets of their game that had let them down last week. Nebraska had only 7 penalties and were 5 of 9 on 3rd down conversions. The Huskers had scored the first touchdown and never looked back as their troubling memories from last week floated off into the distance like the red balloons that celebrated that first score.

Another very relieved man who spoke to the Press was Michael Rose-Ivey, the linebacker who had missed the 2014 season with a serious knee injury and had been suspended by the team for the first game of 2015 because of his violation of team rules. Rose-Ivey led the defense with 10 tackles during the game against South Alabama, and said several times how happy he was to be back on the field. He made light of his misstep when he ran on to the field all alone for the first defensive play, having forgotten that the Defensive Co-ordinator wanted to have a final word to the defense before they went out. It was only after lining up in his position that he realized he was the only Nebraska player on the field. "Oh well" he said "I thought it must be one final punishment for my team violation that I have to play against the offense all by myself".

On a more serious note, Rose-Ivey referred to his violation several times and it was clear that he had owned up to his mistake, accepted his punishment and had worked very hard to work his way back into the team. I was impressed by his maturity, especially in comparison to the professional athletes that we so often see who refuse to take responsibility for their actions.

The third manifestation of relief that I witnessed that evening was not in the press conference but in the stands. It seemed that a gentleman two rows behind me - a season ticket holder from Grand Island since 1992 - had felt a craving for a hot dog since the early part of the first quarter. I could hear him conducting a running commentary for his wife as he kept a keen eye on the vendors who scaled the dizzying heights into our south-western corner of the stadium. His tone of voice grew steadily more concerned as he spotted in turn purveyors of Pepsi, water, popcorn, pizza, Runza's, and candy - but alas no hot dogs. Then as the game continued, the parade of traders would start all over again albeit in a slightly different order. Even by half time there had still been no frankfurting joy in Row 90. What cruel twist of fate, I wanted to know, would keep this poor soul in suspense with a feeling of dogless doom hanging over his head and spreading steadily through the crowd? Did not the Barons of Bratwurst know that they were denying a man who had seen the Big Red through some 23 seasons of ups and downs? Did he not at least deserve the consolation of a soothing saveloy to compensate him for those lean years where so many futile attempts were made to squeeze square peg West Coast offenses into the round holes of the Husker lineup?

But then, it what must have seemed like the vision of a distant oasis to a dying man in the desert, 7 minutes and 32 seconds into the third quarter one brave young mountaineer ascended into the upper reaches of the stadium with his precious cargo. They were warm, they were moist, they were wrapped in foil but most of all they were hot dogs - and above all they were red! As the feeling of contentment spread across the man's face while he and his wife enjoyed their long-awaited reward, I could not help but think life was just about perfect for him at that moment – the Huskers were up 31-0 and he had his hot dog.

The final score: Nebraska 48 South Alabama 9

The Huskers had broken through for their first win and were now 1-1 on the way to Miami.

CHAPTER THREE

THESE BANNERS ARE EXPENSIVE!

Game 3 was to be the Huskers' first away game for the season, against Miami in the Sunshine State. As attractive as the idea of a weekend in Miami sounded to my wife and me, I wanted to stick to my original plan of going to one of the numerous "watch sites" to follow the game. Many people living in Nebraska are aware that there are Nebraska fan clubs all over the country, but they are probably unaware of exactly how many groups of Nebraska ex-pats and other fans gather to watch the game each week.

In Texas alone we have fan clubs known as the North Texas Nebraskans, Houstonians4Huskers, Capital of Texas Nebraskans, and the Huskers of San Antonio. All together there are at least 10 different watch sites spread around the state where Big Red fans gather to cheer on their team. Indeed my first experience at a Nebraska watch party remains clearly etched in my memory.

It was September 2001, just a couple of months after I had moved to Fort Worth. My Omaha-born NU-educated girlfriend (now my wife) suggested that we go watch that week's game at a nearby watch site for the North Texas Ne-

braskans. Up until that time I had only seen the team play on a 21-inch TV in the comfort of our living room, and thus I liked the idea of going somewhere to watch the game on a big screen. Nothing could have prepared me for the experience I was about to undergo, but the number of red vehicles in the parking lot with flags displayed thereon should have given me a hint of what was to come.

The game had just begun when we arrived and walked into a sports bar filled with more than 100 noisy and highly animated fans, every single one of whom was dressed in red. Nebraska scored a touchdown not long after our arrival, and suddenly a DJ operating an elaborate sound system started playing the fight song at high volume. I looked around me at the smiling faces and waving arms as the prelude to the song began, and I could scarcely believe my eyes and ears as the fans responded with their rhythmic clapping and loud yells on cue throughout the song. Their affection for their team was obvious and their enthusiasm contagious. As if this evidence of team spirit was not enough, the seminal moment came when the Blackshirts were called upon to make a goal-line stand and prevent the other team from scoring.

"Let's hear it for the deee-fense!" cried the DJ and 100-plus voices were immediately raised in unison, creating a loud din intended to prevent the opposing offense 600 miles away from being able to hear their quarterback's play calls and snap count. Once again, I could hardly believe what I was hearing and I even said out loud (to no-one in particular) "They can't hear you!" But before the game was over I realized I had missed the point of this raucous display. Cheering for the defense was only a part of the day's purpose, for which the overall goal was to gather with fellow red-clad Nebraska fans and recreate the experience of being at the game and urging on their beloved Big Red. When the friendliness and warmth of the Nebraskan expatriates that we spoke with during the game was added to the lively atmosphere, it was no wonder that my wife and I became regular attendees at these events.

During our various travels over the years we have joined other Nebraska fans to watch games in places such as Minneapolis, Los Angeles and even Honolulu. The latter is worthy of special mention because my wife and I lived in Hawaii for a year, and week after week at the Varsity Bar we would meet a new batch of Big Red fans who had taken time out of their beachside vacations to go watch their beloved Huskers. I was impressed by the devotion that would lead these folks to temporarily trade a lazy deck chair underneath a peaceful palm tree for an uncomfortable chair in a crowded and noisy bar. Even more impressive was the way that many of these visitors from the mainland seemed determined to spend as much time in the sun as possible so that at the next game after their return home their faces, arms and legs would match the color of their Nebraska shirt.

Now back in Fort Worth, we had never watched a game at Flips Patio Grill and so I called the day before the game just to make sure that I was not relying on outdated information when I planned to go there. I wanted to confirm that they were indeed expecting a group of Nebraska fans for the game. Perhaps I was being over-cautious, but I had my fingers burned one day last year when I turned up to the venue and found no red shirts in sight because the game was not being telecast. In any case, my fears were quickly relieved by the young lady who answered the phone and told me I would not be lonely because "Y'all pretty much take over the whole first floor for the game." (I was later to find out that some 250 Big Red fans had come to watch the season opener against BYU.)

After my wife and I arrived we were pleased to see red shirts spread throughout the restaurant, and a number of big screens ready to show the game to the lively crowd. After a few moments a family group originally from Norfolk invited

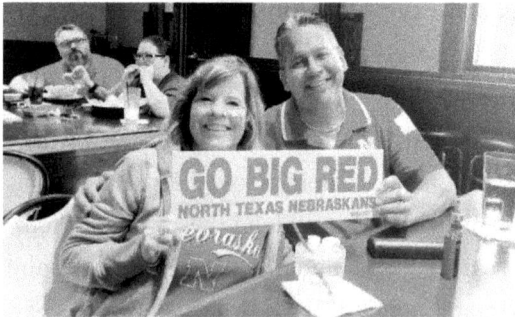

us to sit with them and watch the game, and soon I found myself in discussion with one of the family members about the new coach and the season so far. Thus far along my journey through the 2015 season I have come to understand two things for certain: it's never a challenge to find a friendly face to talk with about Nebraska football, and the owner of the aforementioned face is very likely to have a unique and strongly-held opinion that he or she is more than willing to share.

In this case the owner of the face - a young man of 26 - had invested $200 on the Huskers against Miami and also expressed his doubts about Coach Riley for the long-term because he (Riley) had not been sufficiently upset in public about the loss against BYU two weeks earlier.

There was no shortage of opinions being expressed by others in the early stages of the game as a series of dropped passes and other mistakes saw the Huskers fall behind 17-0 by the end of the first quarter. The shots of the stadium in Miami looked odd at first glance because the seats were only about 75% full even though there were 53,000 fans in attendance. But of course it's a bit unfair to compare that scene at Sun Life Stadium against the appearance of Memorial Stadium on a game day with its 342 consecutive sellouts so far.

Prior to the game starting, the TV cameras had shown a plane above the stadium towing an advertising sign that made us all chuckle. Apparently the Miami fan base is not too happy with their coach who is now in his 5th season, and the banner read: "C'mon. #FireAlGolden. These Banners Are Expensive" This was a sequel to last week's banner that called for the return of its previous coach: "Make Miami Great Again – Butch Davis 2016" But from my point of view, Coach Golden could not have started the season any better, because the Hurricanes began the day with a 2-0 record.

By the time the third quarter ended, the Huskers were behind 30-10 and did not look like getting back into the game. While the game was underway I had taken the opportunity to meet a number of the Nebraska fans, who ranged in age from 6 months to 70-plus. Some fans had left by now, but many stayed on and continued to hope for a Nebraska comeback of some kind. Among those who had stayed were two brothers in their 60s – one of whom had played trumpet in the Nebraska band in his younger days. As a result of always playing the fight song rather than singing it, he had never learned the words properly and was unable to help the rest of us as we tried to sing it after Nebraska's second touchdown of the day brought the score back to 33-18. In any case it all felt a bit futile because with only 9 minutes left in the game, a defeat for the Huskers was clearly on the cards.

I chatted briefly with Alan, another long-time fan, and just before he left for the day he shared his views that 2016's team would be better than 2015. He had heard that Coach Riley was living in a hotel in Lincoln, and he wasn't very happy about it since he felt that it meant Riley was only visiting and not intending to be a long-term coach for the Huskers. However a few minutes later, Alan was back in his seat. He had apparently spoken with a co-worker on his way to the car and was persuaded by him to stay to watch the rest of the game. Just after Alan's return, Armstrong threw his third touchdown with a 21-yard pass to Brandon Reilly and the score was suddenly 33-25 with 4 minutes left to play!

It was riveting to watch as the Huskers had come part-way back from 23 points behind in the space of 5 minutes. They had shown great resolve and character to make a game of it after being all but defeated.

The next possession by Miami would be crucial to the outcome of the game, and the Blackshirts would prove themselves to be equal to the task. They stopped Miami with a three-and-out performance that would have made the "deee-fense" DJ proud. The Huskers used two timeouts and now had the ball back on their own 13-yard line with just under three minutes left to play. In the space of only 100 seconds and without using a timeout, Nebraska used 7 plays to bring the ball all the way to the Miami end zone for a touchdown pass to Stanley Morgan. (Is it just me, or does anyone else want to call him Morgan Stanley?) Financial brokerage houses aside, the score was now 33-31 with a conversion play still to come.

At this moment in the game, long-time Nebraska fans were no doubt reminded about Tom Osborne being faced with a somewhat similar decision when he coached the Huskers against Miami in the 1984 Orange Bowl. But whereas Osborne could have tied the 1984 game with a kick for conversion, Riley had only one minute left on the clock and thus had no option but to try for the two-point conversion.

While the audience at Flips watched in tense silence, Tommy Armstrong threw the ball to Jordan Westerkamp in the end zone for the two-point conversion! Nebraska had somehow found a way to score 23 points in the space of 7 minutes and 59 seconds and the score was now tied at 33!

Just as the overtime period was about to start, with all the reluctance of a young boy who has been told by his mother for the fourth time to leave his game of sandlot baseball and get washed up for dinner, Alan glacially dragged himself out of his seat to go pick up his wife from the airport. Her flight had been delayed earlier in the day but was now on its way. I agreed to call Alan with the result but resisted the temptation to ask whether his wife was a Nebraska fan who might have understood him staying to watch the final stages.

As it turned out, Alan would not have had to stay much longer. The interception of a Nebraska pass on the first play in overtime led to a Miami field goal and a 33-36 defeat for the

Huskers. Although the team was now 1-2 after two very close losses, Coach Riley pointed out to his players in the locker room after the game that they were less than a minute away from being 3-0. They had played some very good football but needed to eliminate the mistakes and penalties if they were to improve their win-loss record from 1-2. Hundreds of thousands of red-shirted fans all over the country were depending on them!

CHAPTER FOUR

COMING HOME TO BEATRICE

*"**Football** is an honest game. It's true to life. . It's a game about sharing. Football is a team game. So is life."*

JOE NAMATH
NFL Hall of Fame Quarterback

Week 4 of the 2015 was Homecoming in Lincoln, and if my wife had been able to join me in Beatrice it would have been a homecoming of sorts for her too. Her mother was born and raised in Beatrice where she attended Centenary United Methodist Church and played trombone in the high school

band. Mary Ann had a gift for music and loved to sing, and although her parents were not well-off they were able to send her to Lincoln in the late '50s to study music at the University of Nebraska. It was there that she met her future husband Tom, and the two were married in 1960.

I always found the story of how they met to be quite charming. Mary Ann was living in the house of her sorority, while Tom was living in the nearby house belonging to his fraternity. It seems that one of Tom's fraternity brothers was dating a girl from Mary Ann's sorority and Tom talked his way into accompanying his friend when he went to pick up his girlfriend for a date. Apparently the pictures of all of the girls in the house were displayed on a notice board in the lobby, and when Tom spotted Mary Ann's picture his eyes lit up. He exclaimed to his friend as he pointed to Mary Ann's picture "That's the one! You're gonna get me a date with her! I don't know how you're gonna do it, but you're gonna get me a date with her!" Tom's friend duly obliged and the four of them went out on a double date. The rest, as the saying goes, is history. Tom and Mary Ann were married for 43 years until Mary Ann passed away.

Mary Ann was a music teacher for the major part of her life, mostly teaching piano to school-aged children from the studio in her home in Omaha. One of her students from an early age was a promising girl named Karrin Schoonover, who showed a flair for improvisation. Now known by the stage name of **Karrin Allyson**, this "promising" young lady has so far had a very successful international career as a jazz pianist and vocalist, having released a number of albums and being nominated for four Grammy Awards.

Looking further up into this distinguished line of succession, my wife and I were astonished to discover that Mary Ann's music teacher – the lady who taught her both trombone and piano while helping her develop her musical talents - is alive and well and living in Beatrice. Joan is 88 years old (what a wonderful age for a teacher of piano with its 88 keys), continues to attend the same Methodist church and still teaches various instruments to a handful of students. And just as important – she and her husband are staunch Big Red fans. They even drive a red car!

When I met the couple, Joan was kind enough to offer me a Huskers t-shirt that was too large for her husband to wear. I gladly accepted her gift but I must admit it has so far done nothing to enhance my musical ability – perhaps I should bring my trombone to the next game and play it from my seat deep in the crowd. A side benefit would be that I could use the slide to jab anyone who is standing up in front of me and obscuring my view of the game.

It has long been my personal philosophy that every day offers the opportunity to learn, even though I have not yet learned to play the trombone that I bought on a whim at the closing sale of a music store in Texas. I knew there would be much learning involved when I took on this project of writing a book about Nebraska and its rich football heritage. However it was not until I visited the Beatrice High School that I began to realize the limits of my football knowledge and that there is so much more to football than simply the game itself.

Beatrice High School sits on the east side of the town, having been built to replace the former high school that my mother-in-law attended which is now the district's middle school. Looking at the ample parking lot I could not help but compare my own high school days in Australia in the 1970s when less than 20 of the school's 1,400 students owned a car. Even more striking is the comparison to Australian high school football where the emphasis was different such that the entire audience watching us play consisted of between 2 and 4 people (our coach, the other team's coach and maybe 1 or 2 fathers who had driven their sons and some of his teammates to the game). Even today in Australia, high school football continues to be a low-key athletic event.

Despite those differences in my upbringing, in my visit to Beatrice I was able to recognize the embodiment of many of the underlying principles that make Nebraska Football so special. I had the honor of being able to sit down with a man who shapes the lives of young men every day. He would never say that this was his job description, but this is what he has done for 15 years and continues to do on a daily basis. Bob Sexton's passion for his role as Head Coach was evident as I watched him interact in a friendly manner with his fellow coaches and his players. His team was heading to Omaha by bus that evening for their game, yet somehow he managed to find the time to show me around the school and introduce me to his coaching staff.

As Bob describes it, four years ago Beatrice had the oldest high school football stadium in the state. Fundraisers within

the community raised some $1.5M towards the cost of a new stadium, and a number of local professionals and tradesmen offered their work for free in the course of building a new facility valued at $15M. Every home game is streamed live on the internet, which allows distant fans such as Bob's mother to follow the team from afar.

We talked about some of the many the life lessons that are offered by participation in a football program, such as the connection between effort and reward, realizing that you can't always get what you want, that you have to play by the rules and accept the decision of the referee, that there will always be others who are greater and lesser than you, the value of playing your role to help the team attain its goals, and so on. I got the clear sense that Bob Sexton was coaching not only football players but also young men and future members of society.

But I am not alone in this view. I was talking to one of the other coaches while they waited for the players to finish boarding the buses to go to their game that evening, and he told me that he was originally from Nebraska but had spent most of his working life in the north-east of the United States. However he never forgot the upbringing he had experienced in Nebraska and as his two sons were getting close to high school age he started planning to relocate back to Nebraska so that they could share his experience in the Cornhusker State. Both boys had showed an aptitude and interest in football, and so their father researched high school football programs that he thought would be most beneficial for the boys. He eventually narrowed the list down to Crete and Beatrice, and after a phone conversation with Coach Bob the family decided on Beatrice.

While we were talking, a couple of concerned-looking players walked back and forth several times from the school

to the bus. Eventually Bob asked them what wrong and they sheepishly replied they could not find their helmets — they had loaded all of the rest of their equipment but the helmets were nowhere to be found. After reminding them that it was their responsibility to take care of all of their equipment, he informed them that their helmets had already been loaded on to the bus. They had apparently left their helmets behind in the weight room earlier in the day, and their forgetfulness was being used as a teaching moment to remind them of their obligations not only to themselves but also to the team who would be short two players if the helmets had been left behind.

I was also impressed by the example of life balance that Coach Bob sets for his players and coaches. On the Friday that we met, he offered me the use of his season tickets for the Huskers game the next day because instead of going to Lincoln he would be elsewhere in the state with his family watching his daughter play volleyball.

Stadium bricks and mortar aside, I felt privileged to have met a man who is working to refine the lives of his students through the crucible of football. Long may he and his program prosper.

While Beatrice High surely has numerous loyal alumni and followers, a number of the many Nebraskans that I have met during the past few weeks have told me about the depth of their loyalty to the Big Red football team. During the past couple of days I have seen and heard that loyalty expressed in different forms.

Everyone who walks into Memorial Stadium passes beneath a sign that displays a statement that helps to explain why the country's longest consecutive sell-out streak is now at 343 and counting. During the 53 years since that streak started, Nebraska fans have only witnessed two losing seasons while the Huskers have won 5 national championships and numerous conference championships. The fans have certainly been rewarded for their loyalty by the team's results over the years and have filled the stadium even on those cold November days when the icy wind blows into town on a non-stop journey from the Arctic via Canada. On such days it must be tempting to stay at home by the warm TV to watch the game, but the sell-out has continued unabated.

Then I heard a story about an individual fan's act of loyalty a couple of days prior to my arrival in Beatrice. The 89-year-old lady, obviously a long-time Big Red fan, had heard that the game against Southern Mississippi would be telecast on the ESPN News channel. During the days leading up to the game she was most perturbed to find that her cable TV provider did not carry this particular station. To not watch the game was of course unthinkable, but exactly how to solve this problem was the question. Perhaps spend the afternoon watching the game with a friend? Or go to the Senior Center? Either of these solutions would have been fine, but the lady in question took a much more direct approach. She simply switched to a different cable company. After all, what was the good of continuing to pay monthly fees to that fool company that didn't have enough sense to make sure that the Huskers game was *always* available to its customers?

On the Friday evening prior to the game I decided to spend some time at the American Legion meeting hall in Beatrice where I hoped to meet a few of the local Husker fans. The presence of 40 or so cars parked outside the windowless brick building was the only sign of life until I walked in to the bar and found it filled with a good number of people mostly over 50 years old, who all seemed to know one another and were enjoying conversations all over the room. Almost all of the seats at the bar were occupied, and one of the two bartenders was kept busy supplying drinks to the half-dozen tables occupied by customers. Red beer seemed to be a popular choice among the table crowd as I watched the bartender pour a healthy dose of cold tomato juice into glasses two-thirds filled with beer. Unfortunately there was no food service on offer at the establishment and so I was unable to order the meal combination of Reuben Sandwich and red beer that would have made my father-in-law proud.

However Tom would have been proud of the Nebraska welcome provided by two different gentlemen who sat next to me at the bar as the night went on. They both bought me a drink during the course of the conversation I had with each of them, but then they each left before I had the opportunity to return the favor. "Welcome to Beatrice" they both said in parting.

I then had the experience of meeting a man in his late 60s who had either possessed an outstanding Olympic-caliber talent in weightlifting and stamina in his younger days, or who now possessed a less-than-perfect memory in his later years. During the course of a conversation between several of us seated at a corner of the bar, this particular fellow mentioned that in his younger days his waist measured 32 inches. The rest of we AARP-age listeners cast our minds back in unison for a few moments trying to remember how long ago it was that our waistlines were that slim, when the speaker continued and said "But of course I worked my butt off in those days". As we nodded in our understanding of that statement he proceeded to explain just how hard it was that he worked.

It seems that in his hard-working days he had been the manager of a local hardware and equipment supply store, and he told us the story of how one day he had unloaded 96,000 pounds of steel by hand, unassisted by anyone else.

My reaction was one of amazement. "That's 48 tons!" I exclaimed.

"Yep" came the nonchalant reply.

This man of average height then explained how he would cradle a 300-pound pack of steel in his arms and carry it to its assigned location in the warehouse. There were also 100-pound packs that he would take, one under each arm, and carry two at a time into the warehouse.

"Yep, I was pretty fit back then" he said while the rest of us sat there still trying to wrap our minds around what he had just told us. It wasn't until I got back to my hotel that I did the mental math on this phenomenal workday. To move 48 tons in 8 hours requires moving 6 tons per hour. This equates to moving a ton of steel, 2,000 pounds to be exact, every 10 minutes.

Given that he was moving the steel in 300- and 200-pound batches, he would have to make a total of four 300-pound trips and four 200-pound trips every 10 minutes. In other words, one trip of either 200 or 300 pounds every 75 seconds for 8 hours non-stop.

And then the question arises that if he was the manager of the store, why was it his job to perform this unloading work and where were his employees while he was doing it? But doing all of this heavy thinking late at night made me tired (and the red beer may have also played a role), so I eventually had to conclude that the passage of 40 or so years must have clouded the memory of my pseudo-Herculean acquaintance.

The next morning dawned bright and clear for the Nebraska game against Southern Mississippi. I had parked my car a couple of miles from the stadium and called an Uber car to bring me to downtown Lincoln. For those not familiar with Uber, this company offers a service similar to a taxi company except that cars are driven by local residents and the entire transaction from request through to payment is handled electronically with credit cards instead of cash. To cite the advantages of Uber vs Taxi as I have heard them described by more than one customer: "Uber is cheaper, the cars are cleaner, the drivers are nice and they all speak English."

I had used the services of Uber two weeks earlier to get me to and from my hotel after the game against South Alabama, but had mislaid my reading glasses on the way back to the hotel. As he dropped me off, the driver Matt promised to send the glasses to me if he found them in his vehicle. As it turned out, Matt did indeed find my reading glasses and then mailed them to me in Texas the following week. They were only a $6.99 off-the-shelf pair from Walmart, but it was a nice gesture for him to not only mail them back to me but also refuse any payment for postage and packaging. It was yet another example of Nebraska warmth and kindness, but as luck would have it I was able to thank Matt in person as he was the driver assigned to me the morning of the Southern Mississippi game.

As I started to walk towards the stadium I reflected on the devotion of the 89-year-old lady in Beatrice who had changed cable providers. Given how the first few games had played out, I couldn't help but worry about her and other senior Big Red fans watching the game. A last-second Hail Mary pass to lose the first game, followed a couple of weeks later by a 23-point comeback in the last 8 minutes to tie the third game and then lose it in overtime. The way things had started out, I was thinking we'd likely see a lot more commercials for cardiologists popping up during the breaks in the game as the season went on.

When I arrived in Lincoln and looked for Bob the ticket-seller, he introduced me to a group of his friends who have a regular tailgate spot in a corner gas station near the stadium. They were very friendly and welcoming, offering me a beer that I was hesitant to accept since it was only 9.30am with the game kick-off scheduled for 11am. But I managed to justify it to myself with the reasoning that if they gracious enough to offer, I should be gracious enough to accept. As I looked around I noted that the gas station was packed with cars and tailgaters, and there was no visible evidence of anyone else being reluctant to enjoy a drink at that relatively early hour.

After taking my leave of the lively group and remembering my concerns about cardiac arrest among the Big Red fans, I was immensely reassured to see a converted ambulance parked near the stadium in preparation for the game. The vehicle had been repainted in the colors of the Nebraska team and sported the word "Huskers" written in large stylized script on each side. Even the word "AMBU-LANCE" which is normally displayed in reverse font on the front of the hood had been replaced by the word "NEBRAS-KA". Obviously this chariot of mercy was intended to support

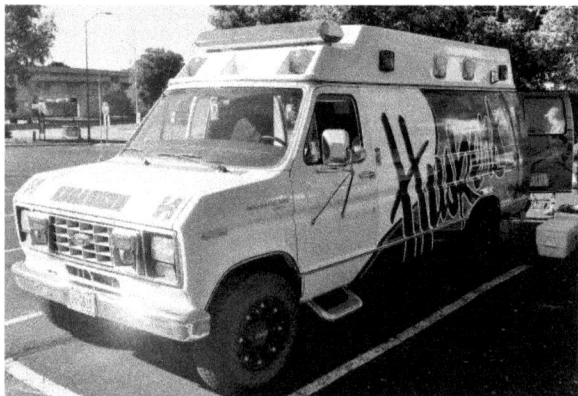

the medical needs of the home team fans, and I assumed there would probably be a couple of more traditionally-attired ambulances to cater to the fans of the visiting team.

However as I got closer to the Husker vehicle I realized that it served a slightly different purpose than what I had first thought when I saw it from a distance. It was indeed being used to dispense some form of over-the-counter medication to the fans in its immediate vicinity, and that exotic medication must have been rather volatile because it had to be kept on ice before delivery to the patient. In other words, I was mistaken in thinking that patients were being treated for heart attacks caused by the fluctuating football fortunes of the valiant Big Red warriors – instead they were being treated pre-emptively to avoid the possible effects of dehydration on a warm day in Lincoln. Those wonderful Nebraska fans: they're just as loyal to one another as they are to their team!

Thanks to the ever-resourceful Bob I secured a seat at the north end of the stadium, and while waiting for the game to begin started talking with the man seated on my left. He had been born in Scottsbluff but was raised in Omaha. He had driven from Denver, where he now lives, and had brought his 6-year-old son to witness his first-ever Nebraska game. It was nice to see the Big Red tradition being paid forward, and both father and son had giant red foam fingers that they happily deployed at appropriate moments during the game.

Once the game was underway it looked like all of my concerns about heart palpitations and fragile senior citizens were for naught, as the home team jumped out to a 10-0 lead within the first 10 minutes. Tommy Armstrong, supported by strong rushing performances from Terrell Newby and Andy Janovich led his team to a 22-0 lead at the half, and the final quarter commenced with the Huskers holding a comfortable 22-point margin with the score 29-7. Meanwhile Fort Worth native Drew Brown had tied a collegiate record by kicking no fewer than five field goals during the first half. Life indeed looked good for the home team as they commenced the fourth quarter with a 2-2 record on the horizon.

But apparently the visiting team had not read the script that was in my mind, as they started to complete some long passes and scored two touchdowns during the first two-and-a-half minutes of the final quarter to bring the score to 29-21. I was hoping that the Husker Ambulance was still standing by as the crowd started to get nervous with mental flashbacks of the BYU and Miami games. But Armstrong relieved the pressure a few minutes later by running in a touchdown to extend the margin between the teams to 15 points with 9 minutes 36 seconds left in the game.

However scarcely more than two minutes later, the sighs of relief among the Husker faithful became constricted gasps as Southern Miss scored their third touchdown of the quarter to bring the score to a fingernail-chewing 36-28 in favor of Nebraska. The 22-point margin had been reduced to 8 by a series of long passes by the visitors and there was still more than 7 minutes left to play.

But as the Golden Eagles lined up to kick off following the touchdown, confusion suddenly broke out among their ranks on the field. Coaches waved their arms from the side of the field and while I watched through my binoculars, the Southern Miss player closest to the Nebraska sideline ran off the field at the behest of his teammates as the play clock continued to tick towards zero. It looked as if the visitors thought they must have lined up with 12 men on the field, however I now counted only 10 after the sudden departure of one of their number. Chaos continued until Southern Miss called a timeout to unravel the confused situation. This would later prove to be a much more important call that it seemed at the time.

After the timeout and subsequent kickoff, Nebraska ran the clock down through a series of running plays interspersed with an occasional pass play. Despite committing several penalties in the process, the Huskers moved the ball down to the Golden Eagles' 7-yard line where Drew Brown lined up for a field goal with 1 minute and 22 seconds remaining in the game. Despite having kicked 5 field goals, this was to be Brown's second miss of the day and it opened up the possibility for victory to be snatched from the grasp of the Huskers yet again.

Making good use of their timeouts while the crowd held its breath, the Golden Eagles marched down the field with a series of long passes until they reached the Nebraska 40-yard line. With 20 seconds left on the clock, the Southern Miss quarterback was sacked by Nebraska's Akinmoladun and precious seconds ticked away. Having wasted a timeout on the earlier kickoff fiasco, the Golden Eagles were unable to stop the clock as they struggled to regroup for a final play. But before they could get lined up, time expired and crowd let out its breath in relief as the Huskers held on to with the game 36-28.

At the press conference after the game I was pleased to see Coach Riley smiling for the first time in a few weeks. The Huskers were now 2-2 and heading to their first Conference game - a very winnable matchup against Illinois.

CHAPTER FIVE

NOT THE VICTORY BUT THE ACTION

The Huskers were 7-point favorites to win their first Big 10 game of the year, on the road against the Illini. I was sure that the Walmart in Beatrice would be deserted for a few hours after 3pm while the game was underway, but I figured there may well be a rush just before game time. Judging by the three nail-biting finishes out of the four games played so far, Big Red fans would need to stock up on over-the-counter tranquilizers and other such products to have on hand to calm their nerves as the game heads into the fourth quarter. In other local news, the 4-1 Beatrice Orangemen would travel to Omaha this week to try to extend their winning streak.

But on game day my wife and I planned to watch the Huskers game at another of the many sites around the country where Nebraskan exiles gather to watch their boys do battle on the field. We looked forward to meeting more Huskers fans and hearing about their memories of the State and its football team. Speaking of fan gatherings, another benefit that I had enjoyed from being among fellow Big Red fans was the sheer quantity and diversity of team shirts that abound. At Dallas Cowboys games over the past few years I have probably seen no more than about 10 different Cowboys shirts apart from the team jerseys. By contrast, in Lincoln and other places I had already seen at least 100 different shirts and was looking forward to seeing more on Saturday at the watch party. My favorite shirt from last week in Lincoln had featured a picture of a certain famous Cornhusker character on the front, and the words "Talk Herbie to me!" on the back.

This week's game also brought up another memory of my wife's father Tom. From time to time at family gatherings, after dinner I would play the guitar while my brother-in-law and I sang the Eagles song "Lyin' Eyes" (yes, there was usually beer involved just in case you were wondering). This particular song was a favorite of ours, but the Eagles and their repertoire of songs with their tight 5-part harmonies had somehow escaped my father-in-law's musical interests which leaned more towards Sinatra and Martin (Dean, not Ricky). As a result, while the pair of we younger ones were torturing those family members not wise enough to leave the room when the guitar came out, Tom always seemed to have a puzzled look on his face.

After having heard our painful rendition several times over the years, one evening he spoke up and asked "Why are you two singing about the Illinois College team?" Now it was our turn to look confused until he asked once more "I mean, who is it that's trying to hide their Illini?" Now we understood that the puzzlement on his face while listening to our song was caused largely by the fact that he thought we were singing the refrain "You can't hide your Illini" when we were actually singing "You can't hide your lyin' eyes".

I wouldn't blame him if there were times when he wished that his daughter would hide my guitar, but as the game drew closer I hoped that the Huskers would render the Illini invisible on the scoreboard at least.

Nebraska fans had of course grown very accustomed over the past 50 years to blanking other teams on the scoreboard, but the inauspicious start to the 2015 season had been a mental reminder that winning is not everything. But there were also more concrete reminders that predated the Devaney-Osborne era.

"Not the victory but the action; Not the goal but the game; In the deed the glory"

These are the noble words inscribed on the southwest side of Memorial Stadium in Lincoln. No such words were inscribed on the walls of Vitty's Sports Bar and Grill in Lewisville, TX but the red-clad patrons enjoying the hospitality of owners Bob and Gayle Vittitoe watched the game in good spirits and with the same intensity normally reserved for game day at the aforesaid stadium. One young man was particularly intense as he focused closely on the large screen in

front of him, loudly offering his advice to the coaches and players after each play that didn't turn out as well as he expected. Perhaps not surprisingly, he had an entire table to himself throughout the game.

Although the marching band was unable to make the trip to Texas, Robert made sure to play "Hail Varsity!" on the juke box after the Huskers scored their one and only touchdown of the day. An even more pleasant surprise was that the song was followed by the passing around of a tray filled with shots of "Hot Damn". I didn't think to ask exactly what was in each little white cup, but the liquid was a satisfyingly appropriate shade of red and we all downed them on cue to celebrate the score. Bob and Gayle are originally from Blair, NE and they obviously know how to make sure everyone enjoys a Husker game. Best of all, my wife and I were seated for the entire game and no-one stood up in front of us!

I'm thinking that the Hot Damn tradition needs to be implemented in Lincoln, although I haven't yet figured out how to quickly get those trays up into the stands after a touchdown and then pass them along the row without an epidemic of red liquid spilling down the back of people's necks. But just in case the logistics of the Hot Damn idea can't be worked out, I do have another proposal that is sure to create some buzz.

The Texas Aggies' tradition is for each man to kiss his date when a touchdown is scored, but my idea is that each man at Memorial Stadium should kiss *someone else's* date

instead. What a great way to meet new people and start animated conversations among the crowd! Especially if you kiss
the date of a fan from the other team!

Before we talk further about the Big Red game against the
Illini, here is some good news from Nebraska. The Beatrice
Orangemen won their game last Friday 20-13, overcoming
three turnovers and extending their record to 5-1. Better still,
unlike the situation in Lincoln no-one is questioning the sanity
of the Beatrice coaches!

The Nebraska game was a low-scoring affair, dominated
by the defense of both teams but at the end of the 3rd quarter
the Huskers held a 13-0 lead. The home team scored a touchdown early in the 4th quarter to bring the score to 13-7. The
teams traded possessions without scoring until just under 5
minutes were left in the game. Nebraska regained the ball and
ran a total of 8 rushing plays while Illinois used all of their
timeouts to try to preserve time on the clock. The clock
stopped with one minute and 46 seconds left when a pass
from Armstrong fell incomplete. It was now 4th and 7 from the
Illini 27, and Nebraska called a timeout to review their op-
tions. The next play would be crucial to the outcome of the
game. Would they try a field goal? Or another running play by
the full-back?

I could do no better to sum up the feeling in the stadium in
Champaign, at Nebraska watch sites all over the world, and in
living rooms across America, than the impassioned shout
from the intense young man at Vitty's that interrupted the
stunned silence that followed right after Nebraska's quarterback threw an incomplete pass with 55 seconds left in the
game: "And you stopped the clock too, you moron!" This was
to be the turning point of the game, but for some reason the

man's emotional eruption at that moment struck me as being funny. Maybe it was the Hot Damn that did it, but it could also have been nervous laughter as I thought the Huskers could not possibly lose from their current position (or could they?) It later turned out that Armstrong had been instructed by the coaches not to risk throwing a pass on that play but instead to run with the ball, following a lead blocker and using up as much time on the clock as possible.

With 55 seconds remaining, the Illini regained possession of the ball and marched down the field to score the game-winning touchdown while we were all left looking at one another and wondering how defeat had been so quickly snatched from the jaws of victory. As one particularly disappointed gentleman said in passing to Robert as he left "Where's the bonfire so we can throw our shirts into it?"

The unexpected defeat must have affected my wife too, because the first words out of her mouth when she woke up Sunday morning were "I still can't believe Nebraska lost that game". But she was not the only one in the house who had suffered from watching the ignominious defeat.

Before we left home to drive to watch the game on Saturday we had left the TV turned on to provide company for Lily, our "miniature husker hound". She had been wearing her white Nebraska scarf at the time, since this was an away game. (For home games she wears her red scarf, of course.)

Given that she is such a fan, we thought it only fair to turn the TV to the Big 10 channel so that she could watch her Huskers in action. I guess she must have watched the game all the way to the sad ending because when we awoke on Sunday morning we found she had chewed her scarf off. It is indeed a sad state of affairs when even man's best friend abandons ship.

The final score: Nebraska 13 Illinois 14

The Huskers had suffered another last-minute defeat and were now 2-3 after their first conference game.

Speaking of conferences, I began to imagine a Saturday morning conversation between the father that I met during the game against Southern Mississippi and his young son who was attending his very first Nebraska game.

Son: Daddy, why did you say the game today is so important?

Father: Well, that's because it's Nebraska's first conference game of the year.

Son: Huh? What was last week's game?

Father: Oh that was a game against another team from another conference.

Son: Oh. *(pause)* What's a conference?

Father: Haven't you finished your breakfast yet?

Son: No, Mommy is bringing me another poptart and some more milk.

Father: Ok, that's great. Go ahead and eat your breakfast.

Son: Daddy, what's a conference?

Father: *(Sigh)* Well it's a group of teams who get together and form a club to play games against each other.

Son: Oh, kind of like when Tommy and me play video games against the Dragons.

Father: Well, kind of like that except this conference is called the Big 10.

Son: But I thought you said there are 11 guys on a football team.

Father: Well yes, there are 11 guys on each team. How's that poptart?

Son: It's good. *(Pauses thoughtfully)* Oh, I get it. There's 10 teams in the conference.

Father: Not exactly, there are 14 teams in the Big 10.

Son: Well then why do they call it the Big 10?

Father: Because they just do, son. The 14 teams are divided into two groups that they call divisions.

Son: Oh, so there's 10 teams in each division?

Father: No, there are 7 teams in each division. Look, how about some nice granola?

Son: Well then why don't they just call it the Big 14?

Father: Well because....er, because that would get people mixed up with other conferences like the Big 12.

Son: So the Big 12 has 12 teams?

Father: Not exactly, the Big 12 only has 10 teams. How's that granola going?

Son: Well then why don't they call that conference the Big 10?

Father: Because that would get people mixed up, too. But anyway, why so many questions about conferences?

Son: It's because Mommy says every time you go to a conference you come home smelling like stale beer and cheap cigars.

Father: Oh, I see. Well just eat your granola, son.

CHAPTER SIX

ANYONE FOR A 59-MINUTE FOOTBALL GAME?

Nebraska's opponent for its second conference game for the season would be Wisconsin, against whom the Huskers' record in Lincoln was 3-0. The Badgers had also lost their first conference game of the year last week, a close 6-10 decision against Iowa who remained so far undefeated. The contest between the Huskers and the Badgers promised to be hard fought, despite memories of a 54-29 drubbing the Huskers had endured against the same opponent one year earlier. But my destination for the days leading up to the game was the intriguingly-named town of Aurora. My father-in-law often talked about the spectacular sunsets in Nebraska, and I clearly recall the background of the car license plates that depicted a beautiful red sky but it never occurred to me to think that the prairie sunrises might be just as captivating as the sunsets they followed.

Aurora is a town of around 4,500 people, located among farmlands some 20 miles east of Grand Island and 75 miles west of Lincoln. But its sunrises are not Aurora's only claim to fame because according to reliable meteorological sources, the largest hailstone ever recorded in the United States landed in Aurora on June 22, 2003: a seven-inch (17.8-centimeter) wide chunk of ice almost as large as a soccer ball. I wonder about the unfortunate soul who was sent out to retrieve that particular hailstone in the name of science in the midst of a storm in which other similar-sized blocks of ice must have been raining down from the sky. It sounds to me like a job for an intern. Or a visitor from Oklahoma.

But that's not all I learned during my stay in Auroras. On the day before the game I met the very laidback Barber Ed, who has a shop in the town's charming and picturesque main

square. While cutting my hair Ed was able to regale me with a couple of his personal memories of the Big Red football program. It seems that Ed's wife's cousin was "Cowboy Ray" Petsch, who was the quarterback of the first Nebraska team to play in the Rose Bowl. In fact this was the first time that Nebraska had ever played in a postseason game. Apparently the occasion of the school's postseason debut was so momentous that classes were cancelled as celebrations spilled out across the campus after the announcement was made. Nebraska had been undefeated throughout the 1940 season except for a 7-13 loss to the number one team Minnesota in the opening game, and as a result the Huskers were invited to play the number two team Stanford in the Rose

Bowl on New Year's Day 1941. Although the boys from Nebraska put up a good fight, they eventually lost 13-21 in front of a crowd of 92,000 spectators.

Ed also told the story of his great-aunt who one day was seated behind the end zone at a game when the ball landed in her lap following a point-after-touchdown conversion. In the midst of the excitement of the moment, the quick-thinking great-aunt immediately though of little Ed and slipped the ball under her coat, hiding it from view. After getting home from the game she gave the ball to Ed, who was of course delighted by the unexpected gift from the home of the Big Red. Ed recalls being amazed when he saw the letters "NU" burned into one end of the ball, which he still has among his possessions. I'm hoping by now that the statute of limitations has expired on the great-aunt's spontaneous crime of opportunity. Ed is by no means a young man, so I'm thinking that the great-aunt herself may have also expired by now.

My wife also has a personal connection to Aurora, since this is where she spent a couple of months in the late 1980s as part of a medical training program and even had her picture in the local paper. Naturally I was very interested to find the photo and associated article, and so I went to the Plainsman Museum to research the newspaper archives from the period in question. But after a couple of fruitless hours punctuated by texts back and forth to my wife to try to narrow down the dates of her stay in Aurora, I had to give up the quest. However I did learn through several advertisements about a contest that was popular at that time among young ladies, namely the contest for the title of Pork Queen. Sponsored by the Nebraska Pork Producers Association, the contest was open to girls aged 16 to 20 whose families worked in the pork-raising industry. The winner would be crowned at a gala event and also be featured in the unforgettably-named Pork Talk magazine.

During this whole search the staff at the Plainsman Museum were extremely helpful and even offered to research further on my behalf after I got back to Texas so long as I could give them more precise dates. When I mentioned in passing the name of the man who had been my wife's mentor in Aurora, they informed me that Dr. Wilcox was still in practice. This was an unexpected stroke of good fortune, and I really wanted to meet this kind man of whom my wife had always spoken so highly.

With hope in my heart I drove over to the town medical center on Friday afternoon and explained to the medical receptionist that I wanted to meet Dr. Wilcox, and my reasons for doing so. I can think of many places in the United States where this request from an out-of-town stranger would have been routinely denied on the grounds of patient privacy, and

other places where I would have been shown to the door by Security. But of course this was Nebraska where I'm happy to say that people are taken at their word, and so the receptionist gave my business card to Dr. Wilcox's nurse who in turn went to see the man himself and explain the situation. Within less than 10 minutes the nurse escorted me back to Dr. Wilcox's office where I was able to spend a few minutes chatting with him. Although he did not recall my wife by name some 27 years and hundreds of medical students after they had first met, I found that Dr. Wilcox was everything my wife had said, and even more than that he's a Big Red fan! (Although of course it could be argued that he is such a nice guy *because* he's a Big Red fan!)

After leaving Aurora on Saturday morning and while driving along I-80 towards the game in Lincoln, I reflected on a couple I had met two nights earlier in Grand Island. They were prominent in my mind because to me they exemplified the link between Nebraskans and their football team, as well as the uncomplicated directness of personality that I find so refreshing in today's hectic world. The husband is originally from Columbus, NE but he now lives in Colorado with his wife. Our paths crossed while we were all having dinner while watching the Thursday night NFL game with one eye and the baseball playoffs with the other.

The pair were on the road because the man's grandmother had passed away in Columbus during the last few days and they were on the way to her funeral. But like all good Nebraskans, Grandma was a Huskers fan. Not only that, she had maintained season tickets ever since 1960. Continuing in the same spirit, the couple was planning to go to Saturday's game to honor her memory.

I am well aware that this whole concept of honoring a loved one's memory through the vehicle of a football game may seem strange to some, but my wife and I did the same thing after her father passed away a few years ago. In this case the Huskers were playing in Washington and there were about a dozen of us who sat in a bar in Omaha enjoying ourselves while looking completely out of place in our formal dark attire as we watched the boys win one for the Gipper. I hoped that the couple I met in Grand Island would be similarly consoled by the game against Wisconsin.

And so it was that 89,886 people (including this happy party of four visiting from Colorado) gathered at Memorial Stadium on a beautiful Nebraska day to watch the Huskers lose the game on a 49-yard field goal with 4 seconds remaining on the clock. Considered in isolation, this last minute loss would be simply one of those things that happens in the ebb and flow of the 11-players-per-team chess game we call football. But when the loss against the Badgers is put in the context of the Nebraska football season so far, it became the 5th of the games played so far that had been decided either in overtime or in the last minute of regulation time. But for a few quirks of fate, the Huskers could have been riding high with a 6-0 win-loss record instead of the dismal-sounding 2-4 position in which they now found themselves.

However the good news was that the coaches and players were determined to continue to fight on and make the most they could out of the season. Emotions were high after the game, but at the post-game press conference Coach Riley complimented his team's ability to deal with disappointments and went on to express his belief that the players would "answer the bell" and come out fighting to get another win on the board the following week. Defensive End Jack Gangwish looked a little emotional as he spoke to the media, clearly having just come off the field with the black face paint not yet washed from under his eyes. Nevertheless he delivered the same determined and forward-focused message that the players would "come out next week firing on all cylinders". Quarterback Tommy Armstrong also seemed very disappointed at the loss, talking in a low voice as he complimented the performance of the Husker defense and assured all present that the team would "keep trying to improve for next week". For his part, Wide Receiver Alonzo Moore (who had earlier scored a touchdown) said "It was a tough loss but we've gotta keep fighting through it".

It was reassuring to see such unflinching and positive attitudes less than 30 minutes after what must have been a heartbreaking loss.

During the final couple of minutes the Wisconsin place kicker had hit the upright on a 39-yard field goal attempt that would have won the game for his team. Gangwish reported that at that point he almost tackled the Defensive Co-ordinator Mark Banker to the ground in his jubilation, feeling that the team had received a new life. But Nebraska went three-and-out on their next possession with Wisconsin using all three of their timeouts during that series. The Badgers thus regained the ball with 1 minute three seconds remaining on the clock and suddenly Gangwish was thrust back into the game to try to preserve the 21-20 lead for the Huskers.

Full credit is due to the Badgers for the way they then moved the ball 42 yards down the field in 59 seconds, using 6 plays and no timeouts. This time the Brazilian-born place kicker for the Badgers made no mistake with his field goal attempt, even though it was longer than the one he had so recently missed.

The final score: Nebraska 21 Wisconsin 23

As hard as it was to imagine in the wake of so many close losses, it was clear that the collective spirits of the Big Red boys remained unbroken and they would strive to bounce back stronger than ever in the next game against Minnesota.

Meanwhile, does anyone know the proper procedure to petition the NCAAF to shorten the last quarter of all Nebraska football games by 1 minute? 5-1 sounds way better than 2-4.

CHAPTER SEVEN

TURNING THE CORNER

While it hadn't been an easy week for Huskers fans, my wife and I managed to cheer ourselves up by demonstrating our faith in the Big Red by getting our curb-side house number repainted with its large red "N" next to the street number. The paint had gradually faded over the past few years, per-haps symbolic of the fortunes of the team during that period, but now our street number would serve as a gleaming outpost of Husker Pride in a sea of Texas Longhorns, TCU and Texas Aggie flotsam and jetsam. Just in case anyone happened to miss the Aggie paintwork on their curb, our next door neighbors were proudly displaying the Texas A&M flag near their front door. All that was needed further was for them to trade in their white SUV for a maroon model.

Speaking of Texas A&M, I have always been intrigued by the school's logo which consists of a large white letter "T" flanked on each side by an "A" and "M", all set against a maroon background. When I first moved to Texas, I did not know that the logo was related to a college and simply thought that the white ATM letters against a field of maroon was indicative of a nearby machine that dispensed money. I later learned of my mistake during a conversation with a friend who had sent all four of his sons to the school. Robert was kind enough to inform me that I had actually visualized the situation in reverse – in fact it was he who was the machine who dispensed money and sent it to College Station.

Aside from the sparkling new display on our streetside, there was further good news to report from our household: Lily the mini husker hound did not destroy her "home team" red Nebraska scarf after watching last week's game with its tragic loss in the last minute of play. (Of course it may have helped that my wife removed said scarf from around Lily's neck before bedtime lest she be wracked with late-night nightmares of long Wisconsin passes down the field that might cause her to take out her frustrations on her scarf in the same way she did after the Illinois game).

Speaking of frustration, however, this poor chap from Scottsbluff got lost while driving to last week's Beatrice High game and found himself in Fort Worth. He was most distraught and kept repeating over and over "I *knew* I shouldn't have made that right turn at York". I gave him directions back to Nebraska and hoped he makes in time for the Friday night game when the Orangemen would try for their 7th win of the season.

But we and all Big Red fans were hoping for a rebound this week against Minnesota. Lily would spend the weekend in a boarding kennel where the other dogs will probably fight it out over which Texas team they get to watch play, but my wife and I planned to join the Oklahoma Cornhusker Club to watch the game at the Thunder Alley Pub in Oklahoma City.

I didn't know whether there would be any political activity outside the bar like there was last week outside the stadium in Lincoln. As I walked across O Street on my way to the game I had encountered a group of students waving "Nebraskans for Bernie Sanders" cam-paign signs and handing out stickers to match. At first glance I thought these spirited young citizens were simply trying to raise public awareness of their favorite Presidential candidate, but after the game had ended I realized that they had a much more important goal in mind in relation to the country's most powerful office.

Many football fans will recall that a couple of years ago President Obama expressed his belief that a playoff system should be implemented to decide the national college football championship, and then suddenly *voilà!* A playoff system was duly implemented. It is abundantly clear that these inspired young men and women have reached a deal with a certain candidate (after all, why else would anyone be seen holding a political campaign sign outside a football game instead of a beer and a hot dog) that his first order of business if elected President will be to enact an Executive Order, applied retroactively from September 5th 2015, that the official length of the 4th quarter of all football games played by Nebraska would be exactly 14 minutes. Once that law goes into effect, the Huskers' record after the first 6 weeks of the season would improve from 2-4 to 5-1 and life would look much rosier in Huskerland.

Now that you've been enlightened on the full story (you're welcome), don't be surprised when you see the players wearing an extra sticker on their helmets for the rest of the 2015 season. And don't forget to play your part in November 2016. Democracy is such a beautiful thing – especially for Nebraskans!

But all of this was in the future. The next order of business was to drive to Oklahoma City and find the weekly assembly place of the local Nebraska fans. As we grew closer to our intended destination I tried to imagine the scene in Minneapolis where my boss had attended the University of Minnesota during the late 60s and described what he called "an invasion by a red army" of Nebraska fans every time the Huskers played against his school.

"You'll have to go around the corner" said the voice on the phone. My wife and I were searching for the Thunder Alley Grill in Oklahoma City and after driving fruitlessly around the parking lot of a large strip mall for about 10 minutes I finally gave up and called the number listed for the establishment (yes Virginia, men sometimes *do* ask for directions). The Oklahoma Cornhusker Club was about to meet to watch the game against Minnesota, and we wanted to be there for the kick-off. After following the bartender's advice to drive around to the back of the mall we found, parked near a blue awning over a door, several of the tell-tale red vehicles that are often characteristic of a gathering of the Husker faithful. Judging from our commercial-looking surrounds, it looked like the door might lead into a large storage space. Instead we found the door led us into a cozy lounge area with a well-stocked bar on one side, and television screens large and small arrayed around the walls of the room.

Several red-shirted fans had walked in before us and more continued to arrive as the time for the start of the game grew closer. None of us knew quite what to expect from the match-up with Minnesota with its 4-2 record in contrast to Nebraska's 2-4 tally, but we all knew we had to be there to watch the game. At the table next to us was a man who had driven down from Scottsbluff to visit his sister in Oklahoma City and take care of some internal family business relating to the death of one of their parents a few months earlier. But like true Nebraskans, they reasoned "What family business could possibly be more important than watching the Husker game together?" The paperwork and rummaging through boxes could wait.

Even though the Huskers were playing away from home against a team with a superior record, a casual observer in the bar would never have noticed any signs of doubt displayed by the loyal Oklahoma Cornhuskers even after the Golden Gophers scored a touchdown on their first possession of the game. The Huskers quickly replied and then after seemingly appearing from nowhere a red-shirted man ran around the entire room with a large Nebraska flag, stopped in front of the giant video screen, and then waved the flag with a yell of "Go Big Red!' that was lustily returned by the crowd.

The only thing missing was the band playing the fight song, but this gap in the celebratory ritual was filled later in the game after another touchdown when a pair of 50ish men played "Dear Old Nebraska U" on their phone while singing along. I congratulated them on their team spirit and told them of my plan at the next home game, where I intend to see who joins me from the crowd while I sing along at top of my voice as the band celebrates a Husker touchdown. I'm not quite sure what the meaning was of the blank look they gave me when they heard this idea - perhaps they were just upset that they hadn't hatched this brilliant plot themselves, or maybe it was that they were carefully studying my face to make sure they would recognize me in the crowd so that they could make certain to sit elsewhere.

The organizers of the Oklahoma Cornhuskers did a great job of setting up the day's activities which included a raffle draw at the end of each quarter, but it wasn't just OKC-based Nebraskans who attended the event. There were several people from the Scottsbluff area (although not the poor soul who got lost on his way to Beatrice last week. I hope he found his way back to Gage County in time for the game Friday night. Unfortunately a 25-yard field goal by with 19 seconds left in the game gave Norris a 31-29 win over Beatrice). There was also a young lady, originally from Omaha, who was visiting from her home in Kansas City. Not surprisingly, the entire group cheered enthusiastically throughout the game and someone even threw a red challenge flag towards the screen after a dubious call against the Huskers by one of the referees. The flag obviously worked because the call was overturned after further review. However I did wonder what would have happened if the original call had been upheld – perhaps we would have all been penalized one bathroom trip during a time-out in the game?

The flag-bearer turned out to be one of the organizers of the group, and during the course of the game he made a point of having a couple of the younger members of the crowd help him on the all-important post-touchdown flag routine. The ages of the audience ranged from around 8 to 80, but all were united in their Husker spirit regardless of the generation gaps we hear so much about in the media.

Corey the flag-bearer has lived in Oklahoma City for a long time, having attended graduate school there. I was tickled to hear him tell the story of a visit home to Grand Island during which he put an OU sticker on the back window of his mother's car as a prank. Well it seems that a few weeks later his mother called him, using the kind of language that mothers generally tell their children *not* to use. Apparently she had been at the mall that day and thought that someone had stolen her car, because she couldn't find it anywhere in the parking lot. She kept coming back to a car that looked like hers but of course could not be *her* car because it had an OU sticker on it.

After about 15 minutes she figured out what had happened and started burning up the phone lines to her son.

Meanwhile the Huskers burned up the field in Minnesota, scoring 6 touchdowns to match their highest score of the year and winning the game 48-25. The fans at Thunder Alley were very happy with the result and so was Coach Riley, on whose face I was glad to see a broad smile in contrast to the concerned and worried expressions that I had seen him wear at several of the post-game press conferences in Lincoln. With only two penalties on the day and a balanced performance from the Big Red offense, it seemed that I was not the only one who had turned an important corner on Saturday.

CHAPTER EIGHT

HISTORY IN HOOPER

As I had done prior to every Husker home game so far, I drove up to Nebraska a couple of days before the clash against Northwestern to spend a day or two in a town to which my wife or her family had some connection. In this case my destination of choice was Hooper, a small town of about 800 people on the Elkhorn River about 50 miles north-west of Omaha. The first thing I thought of as I crossed the Rawhide Creek along the way was the 1960s TV show called "Rawhide", which had Clint Eastwood among its cast members as well as a memorable theme song sung by Frankie Laine. "Rollin', rollin', rollin'" were the lyrics than ran through my head as I crossed the bridge over the stream. I was on my way to find out more about the town where my wife's paternal grandparents were born and raised, but I was also to learn that the origins of the name of creek I had just crossed were far removed from the romantic picture in my mind of cattle drovers crossing the prairie on the way to market.

However I did find a very warm welcome from the good people of Hooper as they offered their help in my quest to learn more about the German immigrant family who had settled and homesteaded in the area in the mid-1860s. Cherie at the Library was most helpful, as was Joyce at the City Office who showed me where I could find the grave of my wife's great-aunt. Reading about the development of the town was an eye-opening history lesson for this Aussie, and I was amazed to think that 150 years ago the area had just been opened up by the advent of the rail line bringing settlers from Germany and Scandinavia while Native Americans looked on.

It was during this early period that a certain band of settlers from Wisconsin decided to travel east to Nebraska to create their own homestead. Apparently one of their number, a foolhardy chap named Easterbrook, bragged that he "would kill the first Indian" he saw. When the group camped overnight on the banks of a small stream, a Pawnee woman walked by with her infant and was duly shot by Easterbrook. It wasn't long before a large group of Pawnee came and took the entire group prisoner, demanding that the murderer be handed over. In due course Easterbrook was handed over, and the Pawnee flayed his flesh raw before eventually killing him.

During the course of a day-and-half I was able to find out that my wife's paternal great-great grandfather Matthias Heller had emigrated from Germany in 1858 together with his wife and young family. The trip across the Atlantic to New York by sailing ship had taken 2 months, which was longer than normal due to adverse winds during the voyage. Unfazed by their recent ordeal, this hardy group made its way to Watertown, Wisconsin where the family attempted to set up farming operations. It seems that this agricultural venture met with mixed success, and after a few years the family began to look for a place where they could buy land of their own.

The Homestead Act of 1862 offered an opportunity for the Heller family, and others like it, to obtain land of their own at a very reasonable price. For the sum of $10 any US citizen (or someone who intended to become US citizen) could claim 160 acres of land in Nebraska, provided he had the intention to improve the property with a dwelling and crops. If the original filer was still on the land after five years, he would receive free and clear title to the property. Matthias decided to make the most of this opportunity and in 1864, his and several other like-minded German immigrant families set out in a group of 13 horse- and ox-drawn wagons to make the 5 week overland journey east to the Hooper area.

When I read about this extended journey, I couldn't help but think of the young children in the group. "Are we there yet?" must have been a common question that these hardy settlers listened to for five weeks as they dealt with wagon breakdowns, river crossings and interactions with potentially hostile Native Americans. And then on the final day when they arrived at their destination with their weary band of youngsters and announced that they were indeed "there", I'm sure the children must have been disappointed to learn that the long-anticipated "there" was in fact in the middle of nowhere!

At the age of 3, my wife's great-grandfather Casper Heller was one of the small children who made the overland journey. He later had 8 children of his own, the youngest of whom was my wife's grandmother Luella who was born in 1898. By this time Casper had also acquired a 160-acre property of his own, some 5 miles from Hooper as the crow flies. Luella rode her horse to school each day and would tell the story of one unfortunate time in her younger years when she set out for school without properly checking the girth on her saddle. Apparently by the time she neared the end of her journey the saddle had slipped around the horse's body and was now beneath its stomach, with poor little Luella grimly hanging on for dear life. Luckily her brother Ben was able to rein in the horse and rescue his little sister from her upside-down predicament. Despite such mishaps, Luella eventually graduated from Hooper High School in 1916. Along the way a friendship had apparently developed with a fellow student named George Hauser who was the son of one of the three doctors who practiced in Hooper at that time. Luella eventually married George and the couple set up home in Omaha.

Returning to more modern times, my earlier disappointment about the lack of a local connection to 20th century TV was overcome by a local connection to 21st century film when

I learned that some of the scenes in the 2013 movie "Nebraska" were filmed at the Sodbuster Saloon in Hooper's Main Street.

Just as an aside, I had so far found that almost every Nebraskan that I met who was living outside the state had seen the movie and loved every minute of it. On the other hand, most of the in-state Nebraskans that I asked had heard about the movie but had not seen it.

Returning to the subject at hand, I would have been puzzled by the name "sodbuster" if I had not read that many early settlers, including my wife's great-grandparents, built their first homes out of grass sod that they dug from their land. In a very labor-intensive process, the walls would be built from rectangular pieces of sod about 4 inches thick, stacked on top of one another, with the internal walls later being plastered (if the family could afford it) and a sheet of muslin being used to provide a ceiling and catch stray insects, rodents and raindrops that made their way through the roof. Not surprisingly, the muslin ceiling would have to be washed every week or so to keep it clean.

While researching the family tree I also learned the origin of another name that had long puzzled me: the Republican River. At first I had imagined that it was populated by fish wearing red ties, and then I decided that perhaps the name was derived from the fact that all of the fish swim on the right side of the river. However it turned out that the name came from the early white settlers who admired the republican-style system of government used by the Pawnee who lived in the area.

Adding to the hardships faced by the early settlers was that the same Elkhorn River which made the area so fertile for farming also flooded periodically, inundating the town and low-lying areas. For example the telephone exchange which had been founded in the back of a grocery store in 1902 was flooded several times and eventually was rebuilt and relocated on higher ground in 1963.

Having worked some 30 years in the telecom industry myself, I was curious to visit the Hooper telephone exchange. There I had the pleasure of meeting Ron the technician who is single-handedly responsible 24/7 for operating and maintaining the telephone system for Hooper and several other regions totaling some 800 square miles.

An arrangement such as this is a far cry from the earlier days when the exchange would have been staffed by several switchboard operators and would have also employed a number of technicians to handle installations and repairs of telephone equipment and the lines that connected the exchange to its subscribers.

Naturally Ron is a Big Red fan, but he informed me he would be unable to watch that weekend's game against Northwestern because he would be watching his son compete in a band competition. With any luck, and if his work schedule permits, he may still be able to find time to compete in the colorfully-named 2nd Annual "Pull My Finger" Chili Cook Off contest scheduled a couple of weeks later.

Speaking for myself, the game against Northwestern actually turned out to be a revelation of sorts. I know I might not be the quickest on the uptake, not the brightest bulb in the batch, not the sharpest knife in the drawer, and I might even have a few kangaroos roaming loose in the top paddock, but after that game I realized that it was time to change careers. That's right, you read it correctly – as soon as the 2015 season is over I'm going to start studying to be a cardiologist who specializes in rescuing people from heart attacks. Of course I'll have to relocate to Nebraska to ply my trade, but there are 1.8 million potential customers there who had their cardiac health severely strained for the first 8 weeks of the 2015 season by the performance of their favorite football team. And who knows what might happen during the following 5 weeks?

The Northwestern game was another perfect example among many so far this season of how the ebb and flow of a football game can elevate the pulse, raise blood pressure to dangerous levels and stress the workings of one's most important organ. Only a person with an ice-cold temperament (or my friend's ex-wife) would not be stressed by the sight of their beloved team losing four of their first six games by a grand total of 11 points.

After the encouraging and substantial victory in the seventh game of the season, the Husker faithful around the country had begun to breathe a little more easily – especially when they were treated to the sight of Coach Riley smiling on the sidelines for the first time. And pulse rates started to stabilize at more normal levels when the Huskers were anointed as 7-point favorites for the game against Northwestern in Lincoln. In case anyone had missed it in the papers or on the pre-game radio shows, a creatively-decorated bus in the tailgate area made clear the expectation that the visiting team would be run over by the unstoppable Huskers

Thanks to my opera-loving ticket man Bob, I was able to observe all of the action from a seat on the 39-yard line in the East Stadium as the Huskers once again provided a 4-quarter stress test for 89,493 people at the stadium and for hundreds

of thousands of others watching on television from the comfort of fine establishments such as the Iron Horse Food and Spirits in Hooper, NE where soothing medication is readily available.

The home team had changed uniforms for the game, wearing all black outfits with red numbers. Unfortunately I had forgotten to bring my binoculars to the game and was unable to identify individual players at a distance due to the low contrast between the black uniforms and the dark red numbers they wore. I was sad for the three siblings of Nebraska I-Back Devine Ozigbo whom I had met at the airport a couple of days ago as we all boarded a plane bound for Omaha. Devine wears number 22 and I was unable to discern whether or not he got on to the field, but I hope his siblings had better luck spotting him than I did.

But regardless of my inability to identify any Nebraska player apart from the quarterback Tommy Armstrong, the game was neck-and-neck throughout. The Huskers began the fourth quarter with a field goal to take a 22-20 lead, and by that point had accumulated 19 first downs compared to only 6 for the visitors. Both teams then had three-and-out possessions until the visiting Wildcats suddenly discovered the ability to move the ball 77 yards down the field in a 9-play drive, culminating in a touchdown and a 27-22 lead. Another three-and-out by Nebraska was followed by a Wildcats field goal and a lead of 30-22. The Huskers took over with 7 minutes and 27 seconds left on the clock, and Armstrong duly led the team on an 8-play drive in the space of three minutes that resulted in a touchdown and narrowed the margin to 30-28 in favor of the visitors.

With 4 minutes and 23 seconds left in the game, pulse rates were once soaring in Huskerland as the home team lined up for a two-point conversion attempt which would tie the game. It was at this point that the idea of a career change hit me right out of nowhere like a sudden coronary attack. After all, if the Huskers were going to keep testing our capacity to handle stress week after week, why shouldn't I be prepared to make a profit out of it?

The ball was snapped and the brute force choreography that is football sprang into action as players from both teams performed their scripted maneuvers of turns, spins and pirouettes while Armstrong danced skillfully away from the defenders who would throw him to the ground if they could. Finally he saw a crack in the Wildcats' armor and launched the ball through a gap towards a receiver in the end zone. But one of the defenders tipped the ball at the last moment and the catch could not be made.

The score remained 30-28 in favor of the visitors, but with 4 minutes and 18 seconds to play, surely the Huskers would get the ball back before time expired? Or before our hearts expired from the stress of holding our breath? Alas it was not to be, as the Wildcats kept possession through 9 plays and were able to run out the clock.

Once again the Huskers had put up a brave fight and ended up on the wrong side of a close finish, having now lost 5 games by a total of 13 points. The boys certainly have nothing to be ashamed of as they have given it their all, and I for one would only be too pleased if their luck would turn and they would put me out of the cardiology business before I even got started!

Go Big Red! (Or Black!)

CHAPTER NINE

NEVER-SAY-DIE
NEBRASKANS

It could never be said that Nebraskans do not go out of their way to enjoy their football. After completing their regular season schedule, the Beatrice High School Orangemen travelled 225 miles in each direction out to McCook in western Nebraska to play their first round game of the Class B State Football Playoffs. In wet and muddy conditions the visitors were down 14-0 late in the third quarter but came back with a touchdown and two-point conversion midway through the last quarter to make the score 14-8. After forcing a three-and-out, the Orangemen got the ball back with just under 6 minutes left in the game. However good defense by McCook led to a Beatrice three-and-out, and the home team were able to run the game out with no further score. Beatrice finished the season with a 6-4 record which included winning 6 games in a row before losing the last two games of the year.

It was a very creditable effort by the Orangemen who not only travelled a considerable distance to face the 8-1 McCook Bisons, but gamely took on the task under difficult field conditions. I was not at the game myself, but the whole event seems to be typical of the loyal, hard-working, never-say-die attitude that has built the Nebraska Territory up from its open prairie homestead days to the prosperous State that it is today. In the same way, this football season has so far been one that has tested the loyalty and resolve of the fans of the storied University of Nebraska program.

After losing the last game, the Huskers found themselves in the unenviable position of having lost 5 games before November for only the third time since 1957. However the game against Purdue who had lost 9 Big Ten games in succession and had so far recorded a 1-6 record in 2015 promised an opportunity for the Huskers to regain their footing. Unfortunately they would enter the game without Quarterback Tommy Armstrong who had sustained an ankle injury in the Northwestern game. He had appeared at the post-game press conference wearing a walking boot but in response to reporters' questions he said that it was "no big deal" and that he was only wearing it for precautionary reasons. Apparently it turned out to be a bigger deal than Tommy thought, and thus Grand Island native Ryker Fyfe would start in his place against Purdue.

This was not good news for the Huskers, since although Fyfe appeared to be a capable player he had only thrown a total of 18 passes during his three years at Nebraska. At the press conference where he announced the news about Armstrong, Coach Riley decided to use a little humor to lighten the air of doom and gloom among the press corps.

"That's the news from Lake Wobegon", he said, referencing the popular show on public radio "A Prairie Home Companion".

The silence in the room was deafening. It was a very awkward moment and I couldn't help but think that it was a stretch to expect a group of sports reporters and presenters from the commercial media to be familiar with a variety show on pledge-driven public radio. Especially when that show plays on weekends during the time that the members of the group in the room are busy working in the world of sport.

Unfazed by the complete lack of response from the audience, he continued "Nobody laughed! Do you even know what Lake Wobegon is?" Fortunately someone did, but by this time the hole Riley had dug for himself was half the size of Nebraska. It reminded me of the time at a friend's wedding reception in a conservative country town some forty years ago when I caught the eye of the groom who was seated at the head table in the front of the room while I was at a table in the rear. Mark and I were only 19 at the time and were apprentices in the same trade school program. In reference to one of our 60ish Instructors who ironically referred to all of us youngsters individually as "Dad", I called across the room "Are you OK over there, Dad?" To me it had been a simple joking line exchanged between two friends, but all conversation in the room came to a sudden and complete halt as 80 heads turned in unison to look at me with stern faces. In my moment of unconscious exuberance I had temporarily forgotten that the bride was expecting. I had dug for myself a hole the size of Australia and I would have been glad if it could have swallowed me up at that moment.

I felt very sorry for Coach Riley in his momentary predicament to which I could so easily relate, but luckily for all of us the conversation soon returned to the matchup against Purdue.

With a 3-5 record entering the game, I was concerned about what the atmosphere would be like at the Flips Patio Grill watch site in Fort Worth. One of the North Texans for Nebraska organizers had previously told us that the crowd numbers had slowly diminished over the season, and we found that by kickoff time there were about 30 Big Red fans in attendance which was down from the hundred or so we had seen for the third game of the season. Although smaller in number, the fans present were no less enthusiastic than normal.

At the table next to my wife and I was a family in which the Omaha-based parents were visiting their son and daughter who both live in Fort Worth. When I asked them about their favorite Husker football memory, they agreed unanimously that the highlight was the game that won the 1995 national championship. While the parents recalled having to move an extra sofa into the living room to accommodate everyone who wanted to watch the game, the younger two recalled the ensuing celebrations in the streets, complete with fireworks.

The game against Purdue began well, with the Huskers kicking a field goal to take the early lead. However this was to be their last lead of the day and by halftime the score was 21-9 in favor of the Boilermakers. Looking around after the long break I could see that only about half of the original Nebraska crowd remained, and the numbers dropped further during the 3rd quarter which finished with the score 42-16. However those dedicated fans that stayed to watch until the end were rewarded with a strong comeback by the Huskers with 4 touchdowns in the final quarter. But Purdue also scored two touchdowns of its own during the same period to make the final score 55-45 for the home team. Fyfe had been very active at quarterback, completing 29 of 48 passes for 407 yards and four touchdowns – however he also threw four interceptions that ultimately sealed the fate of the Huskers on the day. The 7 penalties against Nebraska during the game did not help, either.

Now we had to face the fact that for the first time ever the Huskers had lost 6 games before the beginning of November, and they were also at risk of having only their third losing season since 1961 (the previous two losing seasons had occurred during the Callahan reign). The immediate prospect of the next game against highly-ranked Michigan State made the future sound even more foreboding.

I am far from qualified to express a credible opinion about why the season had unfolded as it had, and in any case my interest lies more in the reaction of the fans than in the specific and intricate details of the events on the field. In my observations thus far I have found there are three main types of fan reactions:

1. Fire Mike Riley and all his cronies!
2. They should never have fired Bo!
3. This too shall pass.

The first group consists mostly of fans 30 and younger. They have grown up watching the team win consistently and go to Bowl games. Winning was expected and any time the winning stopped or even slowed down slightly, the answer was to fire the coach (see Solich, Callahan, Pelini).

As far back as the third game of the season with the unfortunate overtime loss against Miami, one fan shared with me his version of the truth, namely that Riley was really only planning to stay a short time in Lincoln because he was living in a hotel while his wife awaited his return to Oregon. A few weeks later I heard that the reason for the delay was the Rileys needed to repaint the Lincoln house they had bought because of Mrs. Riley's allergies. Another fan shared with me during that same game that he didn't like Riley because he had not been sufficiently upset at the opening game loss to BYU.

The second group of fans seem to be smaller in number and range across a broader age group. The fans I have spoken to in this group all tend to agree that they didn't particularly like Bo Pelini's demeanor as a coach or with the Press, but they all liked the fact that he consistently won at least 9 games every year. Personally speaking, I enjoyed watching Bo most when his younger brother Carl was the Defensive Co-coordinator. Anytime the defense missed a tackle or allowed a long play, the TV cameras captured Bo as he would turn quickly to Carl and give him a look that said "How the $%^& did you let that happen!" Poor Carl in return would look hapless and somewhat guilty as only a younger brother can when his big brother turns to him and asks "Who broke my Batman wrist watch?" I can only imagine what the atmosphere must have been like at the Pelini parents' house for Thanksgiving dinner after each of the football seasons that the two boys coached together!

The third group seems to be the largest, consisting mostly of fans age 50 and older who are able to remember that the Big Red was not always the formidable juggernaut of the Devaney and Osborne eras. Members of this group will say

"Give him time" in relation to Coach Riley, but often continue with "But we ain't gonna wait forever". The prevailing view among these fans is that new coaches and players inevitably need time to get used to one another. Early in the season they were willing to blame the coaches for losses but now this group seems to have shifted more to a view that the players also have to take their share of responsibility for the unexpectedly poor results of the team.

Having pointed out the differences between the three groups of fans, I have seen over and over that there is one overarching principle that unites all groups and all ages – their undying loyalty to Nebraska. They may disagree about what the administrators, coaches and players should be doing at any given moment but there is no question that they would ever shift their allegiance to another team. They are with the Big Red through thick and thin, and neither time, distance nor bad weather can separate them from their beloved Huskers.

And this loyalty, dear readers, is exactly why this Aussie took on the project of writing a blog and book about the 2015 season. I have not only found both the history and geography of Nebraska to be most intriguing, but have also found the unswerving long-term devotion of its people to their football team in today's short-attention-span Twitter-driven world to be very refreshing and quite unique.

CHAPTER TEN

CHRISTMAS COMES EARLY

Judging by the frenzied activity in the electronic and print media that I was able to monitor at a safe distance from Texas, the unexpected defeat at the hands of the unheralded Boilermakers caused quite a reaction from Husker fans all over the country. But before we get to that subject, I saw yet another variation on the Nebraska shirt while enjoying dinner on the eve of the game against Michigan State at the EndZone Bar and Grill in Nebraska City. Up until now, every Nebraska shirt I have seen could be worn almost anywhere. However I would think that the display of this particular shirt is best confined to the four walls of that particular drinking establishment lest its light-hearted message be taken out of context.

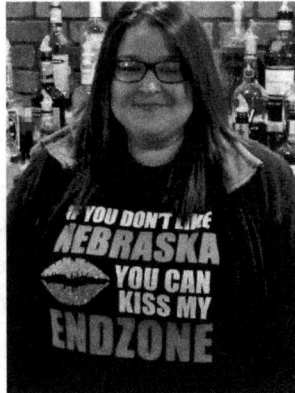

I had been the Husker Hounds in Omaha earlier in the day where I saw an amazingly large range of Husker-related items while seeking supplies for a family reunion of sorts that we have planned in Los Angeles for the final game of the year against Iowa. Although my wife and I have been planning to bring all of our red shirts over to California with us to share with family members so that we can all watch the game at one of the local watch sites in appropriate style, I was feeling that we were still lacking something. Husker Hounds of course came to the rescue with corn necklaces for the ladies, temporary cheek tattoos and various other related items that would be best worn in the appropriate surrounds.

While I was browsing the racks at Husker Hounds it happened that the owner of the store was being interviewed on video for a segment on Fox 42 television. As I understood it, reporter Laura Berry had been doing a series of light-hearted video segments about the current football season and her chat with Scott Strunc was planned to be part of that series. After she had done speaking with Scott, she asked if her videographer could get a shot of me at the counter for background footage. When I told Laura about my blog and book, she decided to interview me as well. Lord only knows what I said to the camera – I just hope that my Aussie accent was sufficiently distracting to cause viewers to simply listen to the strange sounds and ignore the actual words.

Speaking of strange sounds, later that Friday evening I was walking in the main street of Nebraska City and heard the sound of bells playing Christmas music. The streets themselves were deserted – after all it was 8pm by this time – and apparently all respectable denizens of Nebraska City had retreated to their hearth and home by such an hour. It was only a few days after Halloween and it was an odd feeling to hear the music being played for what seemed to be the benefit of myself alone. The feeling morphed into an eerie uneasiness as the cold wind blew through the streets and the bells played the hymn "Just As I Am" which is often played at funerals. I knew the words of the opening verse by heart:

"Just as I am, without one plea,
But that thy blood was shed for me,
And that thou bidd'st me come to thee,
O Lamb of God, I come, I come."

Contemplating the lyrics did not make me feel any less worried, and so I rushed into the nearest bar which was located conveniently close by. It looked like Dinty Moore's had started life as a lunch counter before being converted to focusing more on the beverage side of the product line. There I found a small but animated group of patrons engrossed in playing a simple game in which a golf ball was rolled 10 feet or so along the wooden bar until the slope of the bar caused the ball to roll off the edge on to the floor and come to rest somewhere on a plastic mat strategically placed behind the bar. The aim of the game was for the ball to end up in a designated target zone location on the mat, at which point the player who had rolled the lucky ball would be rewarded from a pot of money accumulated from the $1 paid for each roll of the ball by the various players. As can be imagined, as the night went on the level of skills exhibited by the players seemed to gradually diminish thanks to the fine service from the staff, which in turn caused the jackpot to grow continually larger. During my stay of less than one hour the jackpot must have grown by some $30-40 without any of the players even getting close to the winning zone as far as I could tell. But I was relieved to find that the mysterious music had concluded by the time I left. Even more importantly I had enjoyed a good conversation with John the official game judge, who thought he may be able to get me in touch with well-known Husker fan Larry the Cable Guy.

My feeling of uneasiness had long since dissipated by the next morning but I experienced a flashback to the night before when I walked into the local Walmart where many Christmas decorations were already in place, highlighted by a large wreath hanging from the ceiling of the store. I had gone there to buy the local and Lincoln newspapers, only to find that the store did not stock newspapers of any kind. (My country newspaper editor grandfather would be rolling in his grave at such news, or lack thereof.) But as I left the store I understood the problem that caused the premature decoration – how on earth were the managers supposed to find out that Thanksgiving was still three weeks in the future if there was no newspaper to inform them? The Happy New Year 2016 signs would probably be on display by the time the turkeys were being cooked.

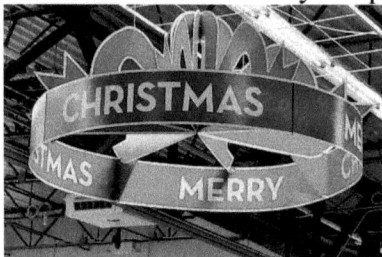

When I finally did find a newspaper (at a gas station, where else) I read a number of responses to the current 3-6 Husker situation. The Lincoln paper carried a couple of letters to the editor in which one of the writers argued that this season was better than most because the games were more interesting and exciting than normal. Every point counts this year, as opposed to previous years in which the only excitement in the game was predicting the size of the eventual Husker winning margin. On the other hand, the local Nebraska City paper carried an opinion piece in which the author argued that the current series of events may cause Big Red fans to lose interest in the team during the coming lean years as the team rebuilds. This negative mindset of assuming several bad years to come, and the assumed diminished loyalty to the team were both contrary to what I had so far found among the folks I had met throughout my Nebraska travels. Nevertheless in times such as this, comic relief from Larry the Cable Guy would be most welcome!

Such comic relief had been at hand earlier when I met Ray on my flight from Denver to Omaha. Ray is a Nebraska native who was on his way from his home in Oregon to visit his family in Omaha. Since he lives in Oregon, Ray had long been familiar with Coach Riley while he was at Oregon State and he made me laugh out loud when he drew a comparison with Mr. Rogers. When I asked Ray about his favorite Husker memory, he recalled the 1995 National Championship game in Arizona against Florida. Not only was Ray at the game, he jumped the fence in his jubilation after the win and ran on to the field. Not content with just being on the field, he proceeded to photo-bomb a number of the post-game TV interviews with coaches and players, jumping up and down and waving his arms in the background while being seen by a number of his friends watching the game at home. Surely no jury in the world would convict a Nebraska fan for trespassing on the field after winning a national championship, but I hope he had not told his boss he was staying at home sick that day!

Coach Riley may not have been laughing Saturday night at the post-game press conference, but he was certainly smiling from ear to ear as he opened the meeting by saying "I guess we found out it's not over 'til it's over". He was referring to Nebraska's stunning last-minute one-point win against the number 6 team in the nation, the previously-undefeated Michigan State Spartans.

Judging by the scenes of pandemonium a few minutes earlier at the end of the game as the Nebraska players and coaches ran on to the field to the roar of the ecstatic crowd of 90,094 people, one would be forgiven for thinking that the Huskers had just earned a trip to the Big 10 championship game. But while there was no formal trophy for the thrilling victory, the team won redemption for itself and its coaches as for the first time this year they were the victors in a close game that came down to the final seconds.

The game had been fairly even throughout, with the Huskers leading until just before the half. However the highly-favored Spartans pulled away during the third quarter to take a 31-20 lead with 15 minutes left to play. With just over 4 minutes remaining in the game, the Huskers got the ball back after a Spartans touchdown that had made the score 38-26 in favor of the visitors. It was a cold evening in Lincoln and many people took the opportunity to leave the game at this point, thinking that the plucky Huskers had reached the point of no return. But quarterback Tommy Armstrong led the team on a 10-play drive that ended with him running in his second touchdown of the night.

The ball went back to the Spartans with less than 2 minutes remaining with the score at 38-33 and the odds stacked heavily in their favor. Thanks to a solid three-and-out defensive performance by the Huskers and the use of its two remaining timeouts, the Huskers got the ball back on their own 9-yard line with 55 seconds remaining on the clock. Armstrong immediately went to work with two long pass completions to Westerkamp to bring the Huskers to the Spartans 30 –yard line. After an incomplete pass, he threw a 30-yard pass to Brandon Reilly for the go-ahead touchdown to bring the score to 39-38 in favor of the home team. Husker fans held their breath as the touchdown play was reviewed, since Reilly had stepped out of bounds and returned to the field before catching the ball. However the final ruling was that he had been forced out of bounds by the defender and thus the touchdown play stood.

It was a remarkable drive down the field and in fact it was almost too efficient as it left 17 seconds on the clock for the Spartans to try to get into field goal range. Once again the defense held firm in the face of the Spartans onslaught and the Huskers ran out winners by the narrowest of margins.

While the players ran on to field to celebrate, their jubilant fans stood in place and roared their appreciation of a remarkable performance by their Huskers. I can only pity those who had left the stadium with the score at 38-26 and were hearing roars as they walked to their cars, followed later by descriptions of the heroics over the radio. If only they had followed the same guiding principle as Coach Riley when it comes to deciding when a game is truly over they would have witnessed some remarkable scenes of jubilant Husker fans hugging and celebrating the David and Goliath-like victory.

For happily obvious reasons, the post-game press conference was completely different to those after all other games so far this season. Coach Riley was as usual the first person to face the media, and it was good to see him smiling as he talked about how happy he was for his players and coaches. He admitted that he had not had a good view of the crucial touchdown play by Reilly at the end of the game and had thought that the on-field decision would be overturned. (I was tempted to ask him if he had considered throwing his red challenge flag when the ruling on the field was upheld. I'm sure my question would have got a laugh from him and the 20 or so journalists and reporters in the room but it may also have got me shown to the door and issued an invitation not to return to future press conferences.)

While the review of the play was underway, he and the other coaches were drawing up other plays they could run from the 30-yard line during the 17 remaining seconds of the game. Riley was clearly very pleased with the result of the game but handled it in the same calm manner that he has displayed throughout the season. He refused to be drawn into speculation about what the victory may mean for the future, saying only that it was "Good for right now for this group of players".

In my opinion, Coach Riley's 10 minutes in front of the assembled cameras and reporters provided a great deal of insight into the man in charge of the Huskers football team. We learned that rather than being reactive and impulsive, he faces both victory and defeat in a level-headed manner and with a long-term view.

Rather than ranting in the ear of a sideline referee during the review of Nebraska's critical touchdown play as some coaches would have done, he was huddled with his team planning for the next steps to win the game.

Rather than getting overly caught up in the moment after the team's triumphant win, he was keeping his eyes on the remainder of the season. I have seen him looking and sounding upset for his players after some disappointing losses this year, but after this game it was clear he was enjoying the way his players were feeling. A number of fans that I had met so far this year had misinterpreted Riley's unflappability as a sign of lack of personal commitment to Nebraska, but after the Michigan State game it was clearly demonstrated for all to see that he is unflappable by nature, and is fully committed to the Huskers for the long haul.

Nate Gerry, Imani Cross and Brandon Reilly all had big games for the Huskers and answered questions from the media. All three of them spoke about how this particular game would live long in their memories. When Cross was asked how it felt to come on to the field with 91 yards to go with 55 seconds remaining, he said he didn't feel that task was impossible. "We do it all the time in practice", he said. I hoped that those fans who had been criticizing the coaching staff would take note of that statement and the evidence that backed it up to the tune of 91 yards in 38 seconds.

When quarterback Tommy Armstrong took the podium, I could not help myself from asking the first question. I wanted to know how was he able to keep his cool throughout a roller - coaster ride of a game when some sections of the crowd booed when he threw an intercepted pass on 2nd and goal, and later on when the same crowd cheered him wildly for his final two drives of the game. He responded in very mature fashion, saying that he tunes out the crowd noise and just focuses on his teammates in the knowledge that they are very capable of getting the job done together. He praised his teammates several times in response to other questions, deflecting any praise from himself. As was the case with his head coach, I felt that this performance in front of the media by Armstrong revealed much about the character of the man facing the cameras.

But I'm sure than none of the dedicated fans that I had the pleasure of meeting on game day were among the ranks of those who booed the intercepted pass. During the space of a few hours before the game I had the opportunity to meet fans who had traveled from as far afield as Huntington Beach CA, Phoenix AZ and Las Vegas NV, not mention many different

parts of Nebraska. Just as the Huskers were in the process of a transition of coaches, there was also a changing of the guard among the fans as the older folks slowly make way for the more elaborate stylings of the younger brigade. The overall-clad threesome in the back-ground of the photo had driven 5 hours from western Nebraska for the game, a journey they undertake once per year.

Earlier in the day Bob the opera-loving ticket man had in-troduced me to some friends of his in the gas station tailgating area near where he plies his ticket trade. In typical Nebraska style I was warmly welcomed and enjoyed Jen's fabulous chili, red velvet cinnamon buns, brownies and other assorted delicacies. Tailgating in the 21st century is a far cry from ear-lier years judging by the sophisticated comforts of home that

Jen and her husband Mike brought with them to the gas station-based space they have occupied for the past 7 years. They have it down to a fine art as the truck (red, of course) is

driven inside the garage, the TV is plugged in to the satellite dish mounted on the roof for this very purpose, and electric casserole dishes are plugged into power sockets. As if that were not enough, the couple next door to them brings a complete spirits-based bar set-up complete with exotic garnishes for the drinks that they prepare for the pre-game revelers.

There was a real spirit (no pun intended) of camaraderie throughout the area as people shared food and drinks with one another in addition to their predictions of a possible upset in the game against the highly-rated Spartans.

Speaking as we were earlier of transitions, judging by the way one particular gentleman in the tailgate crowd was dressed it appeared to be in the midst of a seasonal transition, in the process of morphing from a summery red Elvis to a more wintry Santa.

Among the other Big Red fans who had traveled from afar were Bobby and Gayle Vittitoe, who own and operate Vitty's Bar and Grill in Lewisville TX. This is one of the official watch sites for the North Texas Nebraskans, and the location where I watched the Illinois game complete with Hot Damn shots. Like the many other Husker fans who selected in advance the Michigan State game as the only one of the season that they would watch in person, I'm sure Bobby and Gayle were grateful for having chosen the right weekend for their annual pilgrimage to Memorial Stadium

But prior to joining the tailgating crowd I also had the pleasure of meeting a nice Michigan couple before the game bar of the Holiday Inn.

This retirement-age pair had driven 12 hours from Michigan to Lincoln to watch their first-ever Huskers game. We had a nice conversation as I warned them that they would likely be herded into a green ghetto in one corner of the stadium from which they would be able to see their fellow visiting fans as an island of green in the diagonally-opposite corner amidst the sea of red. After suggesting they might want to take the opportunity to rent a seat cushion to make themselves more comfortable during the game, I inquired about their return trip to Michigan. They told me that they would break up the trip by spending a night in Chicago with their son and his family who live there.

"How nice" I said, "that will be a happy moment in what will otherwise be a very sad trip home after your team loses to Nebraska."

My comment was of course intended in jest, but even as I uttered those words I couldn't help but feel a little bit guilty for teasing these nice visitors like that. But in the immediate aftermath of the game, I must say I didn't feel guilty at all!

Later that night after I thought more about it while lying in bed, I had trouble sleeping – not because of a guilty conscience about spoiling that nice couple's mood but because of another prediction I made last year.

I had written the script of a musical comedy for a local theater group in Fort Worth, in which the show was set in 2019. According to the story, President Trump was in charge of the country and one of his first acts of office had been to sell the Washington Monument to real estate developers who turned it into a high-rise condo building. But that's not the part that made me lose the most sleep – I had also predicted that his Vice-President was Dallas Cowboys owner Jerry Jones. After reviewing the frightening implications of that scenario I resolved to steer clear of predicting politics and reserve my prognostications for more gentlemanly sports like football where at least they have a rulebook to play by.

To help put the Huskers' exciting and memorable win over Michigan State into further context, I'd like to share my observations about some of the things that were different about that game in comparison to the games earlier in the season.

The Home Crowd

Maybe it was the pre-game Veterans' Day salute to our men and women in uniform past and present, or the aircraft flyover, or that the crowd could smell the possibility of an upset brewing, but whatever the reason may have been, the crowd was boisterously involved in the game from the very beginning. Of course the home crowd at Memorial Stadium is always loud and proud, but for this game they were even more responsive than usual which I'm sure must have made an impact on the Nebraska players. The crowd remained emotionally involved throughout the game, even to a fault when some sections booed the 3rd quarter pass interception near the Huskers' end zone.

Nothing to Lose

It goes without saying that the Huskers players have given their best throughout a challenging season studded by a series of heartbreakingly-close losses. Speaking for myself, it had not been a pleasant sight to witness the emotional pain on the faces of the coaches and players at the post-game press conferences as they answered questions about what went wrong and why they lost particular games. But at no point did I sense any feeling from the coaches or players of resignation or giving up on the season. On the contrary, they always talked about starting each new week with a fresh and determined approach.

What was different in the Spartans game was that the players somehow raised their effort to a whole new level. To me it appeared that they played as if they had nothing to lose. Not to denigrate their effort in earlier games in any way, but they played against the Spartans like men possessed. Just to cite one example, no-one who watched the game will soon forget the performance of Wide Receiver Jordan Westerkamp with his 9 receptions for 143 yards and 1 touchdown. While he made his touchdown reception look easy, most of his other catches were made under strong pressure at the expense of his own physical safety. He came out of the game at one point after injuring himself yet returned later to make some key receptions including two long passes down the middle of the field during Nebraska's final game-winning drive.

Balanced Offense

The Huskers established the running game early on thanks largely to the efforts of Imani Cross. This in turn opened up the passing game and allowed for a much more balanced offense that we have seen in some of the earlier games. Led by Cross with his 18 rushes, with 7 more from Armstrong (including two rushing touchdowns) the Huskers racked up 34 rushes for 134 yards. Meanwhile the passing game consisted of 39 pass attempts of which 24 were successful, for a total of 348 yards and 2 touchdowns. Those results speak for themselves and together with ever-present threat of Armstrong using his feet to gain yards, the Spartans defense was kept off-balance for the whole game.

- Cold Weather

I don't know whether the cool temperature in the 40s affected the Nebraska players but it certainly had an impact on your intrepid Aussie reporter. Even though I had wisely ingested some small portions of warming fluids before the game, I was nowhere near as well-fortified as many of the 90,094 fans who braved the windy and body-heat-sapping conditions.

Reaction of the Upstairs Coaches

The spacious and well-equipped Press Box is located on the 6th floor of the West Stadium, along with a number of private suites reserved for Nebraska coaches as well as coaches of the visiting team. My habit throughout the season has been to buy a ticket to the game so that I can watch the game from somewhere amongst the crowd and listen to their reactions, but I always return to the Press Box for the final few minutes. A few minutes after the game concludes, I normally see the "upstairs" Nebraska coaches leave their boxes and head towards the elevators. So far this season the post-game parade of coaches has been somewhat similar to a funeral procession as they walk slowly together in silence, solemn-faced and deep in thought.

After the Michigan State game I almost missed the parade of coaches because they bolted out of their boxes right after the final whistle and ran down the hallway hooting and hollering like teenagers in a hard-earned and well-deserved celebration of a remarkable win over the undefeated Spartans. Their mixture of joy and relief was so infectious that I almost wanted to join them.

While many things were different for the Michigan Stage game, it's worth noting some that had not changed.

Players Belief in Themselves

While the players who spoke to the media after the game were clearly happy about their historic win, they continued to express a sentiment that had been a constant presence throughout the season: namely their belief in themselves, their teammates and their coaches. They had worked hard all year and kept the faith, and now finally they were rewarded in spectacular fashion by their victory over the nation's sixth-ranked team. A just reward, if ever there was one.

Willingness to Fight Back

The Huskers had been down during many games this year, but they had never counted themselves out. They had fought back from very difficult positions in several games this year, including scoring 29 points with a backup quarterback in the 4th quarter against Purdue one week earlier. That same spirit was clearly evident from both the Huskers offense and defense against the Spartans as the Big Red fought back from a 12 point deficit in the final 4 minutes of the game.

While some things were different in that game and others were not, we could all be assured that the remaining two weeks of the season would be even more exciting than all of the previous ten weeks combined. Perhaps the managers in the Nebraska City Walmart knew something that no-one else did, because Christmas indeed came early for all Husker fans with that exciting win over the Spartans!

CHAPTER ELEVEN

NOT IN NEBRASKA ANYMORE

As if the pleasantly surprising and unexpected events of the prior Saturday had not been enough, on the following Monday my wife received a call from her Omaha Westside High School friend and former UNL college roommate Kathy who now lives in New Jersey, to inform her that she and her husband had just been given 4 tickets to the coming Rutgers game. Would we like to join them at the game, was the question. After spending several milliseconds deep in thoughtful deliberation we gladly accepted, and thus we cancelled our plans to go watch the game at a Huskers watch site in St. Louis and instead made plans to go watch the Huskers visit High Point Solutions Stadium for the first time as they faced the Rutgers Scarlet Knights.

Both teams would be playing for the eventual chance to go to a bowl game, however both teams had already lost a number of games and needed to win to give themselves a chance at a .500 season. The winner would keep its hopes of a 6-6 season alive while the loser would be consigned to doing no better than 5-7 for the year.

While Rutgers had been to a bowl game in 9 of the last 10 years, Nebraska had played in a total of 51 bowls which put it third on the all-time list behind Texas (53) and Alabama (62). Since both teams had a strong incentive to win, the game promised to be a hard-fought affair.

The fact that we were making our reservation to fly from Dallas to New Jersey only a few days ahead of our intended departure date meant that we were unable to fly to our chosen destination of Newark without taking out a second mortgage on our home. Instead we were able to fly to La Guardia which also offered the unexpected bonus of an extended late-night drive through the suburbs of New York and New Jersey complete with practically unlimited close-up views of wall-to-wall semi-trailers.

The good news for my wife and me the next morning as we got ready to go to the game was that the day was sunny and had already reached its maximum predicted temperature.

The bad news was that the aforesaid maximum predicted temperature was 48 degrees. The four of us decided unanimously that we may need to supplement our pre-game preparation with some internal thermal fortification just before the kickoff so that we might cheer for the Huskers in suitably spirited style.

At precisely 2.35pm my wife and I pulled into the parking lot at High Point Solutions Stadium with our friends Kathy and Bill where we encountered a typical pre-game scene filled with red-clad fans enjoying themselves with their usual tailgating activities. Bean bags were being tossed, smoke curled upwards from portable grills, the occasional football bounced across the ground between the parked pick-up trucks, and a group of animated fans were enjoying themselves near a converted red school bus as they supplemented and maintained their hydration levels. The sun was shining and families were having fun together on a sunny afternoon during the football season. Red flags adorned with a single white capital letter fluttered overhead and the faint sounds of upbeat music occasionally drifted across from a distance.

We sat in the car for a few minutes, taking in the scene and enjoying the ambience as a handful of 30ish men set up folding chairs near us while they talked about the coming game and continued the all-important intake of fluids in preparation for the 10-minute walk to the stadium. In short, it was an idyllic scene of Americana, typical of many that I had witnessed during the past few months.

The first hint of something being amiss came when one of the nearby men

turned towards us and I noticed that his red cap was adorned in white not with the letter N, but with a large letter R. My eyes quickly scanned his friends and found that they too had the same sinister letter R emblazoned on their shirts. In panic I turned and saw that the nearby red flags waving in the breeze also had the same inexplicable R. There was only one explanation for it – we had entered <*dramatic pause*> The Twilight Zone. <*Cue music: dee-de-dee-dee, dee-de-dee-dee*>

The inescapable conclusion was that we had landed in a parallel universe where although many things looked very familiar, there were differences in key details. Upon getting out of the car we realized that although the sun was shining, it was projecting almost no heat. As we walked towards the stadium, we at first thought we heard people shouting "Go Huskers!" but they were really saying "Go Rutgers!"

Once inside, we found the stands filled with good-natured and friendly fans dressed only in red yet most were wearing the ubiquitous and cult-like letter R. We knew that some of our Nebraska comrades must also be in attendance but from a distance they were indistinguishable within the crowd of 45,606. We heard that Husker fans were indeed sprinkled throughout the red crowd, but how to find them?

Whatever happened to the orderly certainty of Memorial Stadium where the visiting team's fans in their contrasting colors are summarily herded into two small ghettos in opposite corners of the stadium amidst the sea of red? We could see Herbie Husker on the other side of the stadium, bravely executing his usual shenanigans along the sideline in front of the fans but where was Li'l Red? (We would later find out that he had been detained by Security at Lincoln airport for refusing to remove his red cap for the TSA agents.)

After finding our allocated seats we were comforted to find that they consisted of the satisfyingly cold and hard aluminum planks that we were so used to enduring, but they also included something never before seen in Lincoln called a backrest. As if the built-in backrest were not enough unaccustomed inconvenience, we were also disconcerted to find that the seat width allocated to each person was several inches wider than in Memorial Stadium. How could we possibly focus on watching the game if we were comfortably seated without knees in our backs and neighboring elbows jabbing into our ribs? All I could think was "Gosh Herbie, it looks like we're not in Nebraska anymore".

The temperature had soared to 49 degrees by the time of the kickoff and although I had bought a program for the game, I seldom consulted it because I was too busy using it to insulate my backside from the cold seat. Early in the game before the sun disappeared behind the video screen at the western end of the stadi-

um and gave way to the twilight and plummeting temperatures, Huskers tight end Cethan Carter took a handoff from Armstrong 32 yards down the sideline for a touchdown and an early lead. Not only was this the first-ever rush by Carter during his college career but it was also the first rush attempt by a Nebraska tight end for the last four years. I told you we were in the Twilight Zone!

During a timeout early in the game the large face of a man appeared on the video screen and was greeted by loud boos from the home crowd as he talked about a charitable cause of some kind. I had been talking with the Rutgers fan seated next to me and so I simply asked him whether they were booing the man on the screen or the cause he was promoting. Since we were in the Twilight Zone I should not have been surprised when Jonathan informed me that it was the man who was being booed, and that the man in question was the Rutgers Head Coach. Of course – who else would they be booing? *<dee-de-dee-dee, dee-de-dee-dee>*

Later in the game Carter would score a receiving touchdown, one of three thrown for the day by Tommy Armstrong. As the game wore on I decided to run a test to explore the limits of the Bizarro world in which we found ourselves. During a period of relative silence following a touchdown by Nebraska I cupped my hands and cried out at the top of my voice "GO   BIG   RED!" As every red-blooded Husker fan knows, the standard response to that stimulus is a multitude of voices shouting in unison "GOBIGRED!"

But all I could hear in response was the chirping of crickets. And, in my mind, music: *<dee-de-dee-dee, dee-de-dee-dee>*

Nebraska stayed in front throughout the game and ran out 31-14 victors, even in the face of a trick play by Rutgers during the third quarter when wide receiver Janarion Grant threw the first touchdown pass of his career to his quarterback Chris Laviano.

It had been a day filled with firsts, as Nebraska won its first-ever game at the home of Rutgers in Piscataway, and for the first time I saw a pair of penguins in the stands as they danced happily around the ice-blocks that used to be my feet.

The performances of the past two weeks by the Huskers had shown that they were clearly capable of beating the undefeated Iowa in their next contest and bringing their subsequent 6-6 record to a Bowl game. My vote would be to go to the

Pineapple Punch Bowl in Honolulu – I like the Tropical Zone much better than the Twilight Zone!

CHAPTER TWELVE

CALIFORNIA DREAMING

The weather forecast for the game against Iowa on the day after Thanksgiving was not very inviting, to say the least: 28 degrees, for heaven's sake. I figured those Nebraskans must be made of stern stuff to contemplate standing out in the cold like that to watch their boys in red take on the nation's fourth-ranked team, and an undefeated team at that. But knowing the loyalty of the home fans, I had no doubt that the long-running sellout streak of more than 50 years would continue despite the weather conditions. As for me, this was to be the only home game of the year that I would miss, since my wife and I had long planned to spend the Thanksgiving Holiday period with her family in the Los Angeles area where the forecast for that same day happened to be a much more civilized 63 degrees.

On my last trip to Nebraska I had made sure to stock up on Nebraska accessories for this very trip as there would be up to ten of us watching the game along with the other Big Red faithful at one of the official Californians for Nebraska watch sites. As I had tried to explain to some visitors from Sweden would be in town at that time, the price of admission to a Husker watch party is being dressed appropriately for the occasion. After all just as it would be dreadful etiquette to attend a formal wedding attired in jeans and sneakers, to go to a Nebraska watch site without wearing copious quantities of red and all manner of related accessories would be completely out of place. Fortunately the capable crew at Husker Hounds in Omaha were able to make sure I got what I needed, which included a new hatband for my Panama hat, corn necklaces

for the ladies and a couple of packages of temporary N cheek tattoos. My wife and I also brought with us to California our spare Big Red shirts, while my nephew who is home from college arranged to bring his corn cob hat with him. We also planned to assemble the entire clan outside the bar for a final inspection before going in to battle against the dreaded cross-border foe, just to make sure that all present were in correct uniform.

On another note, I must say I never cease to be amazed by the sheer number of Nebraska fan clubs spread across the country. When searching online for a watch site for this particular game, I found no less than five such locations within an hour's drive of our temporary California home. And I was sure that each would be populated by fans dressed in all manner of Husker attire, hoping for a repeat of that fabulous feeling from a few weeks earlier when the Huskers beat the highly-ranked and undefeated Spartans in a thrilling finish. I will never forget that moment when the game ended: the players streamed on to the field and the fans in the stands just went wild with their jubilation, dancing, hugging, high-fiving, singing and yelling at the top of their lungs.

A result like that against Iowa would surely set the hearts of Nebraska fans everywhere on fire, regardless of what the thermometer outside was saying!

In recognition of the importance of the occasion for the Huskers when they took on the undefeated Iowa team, Lily the mini husker hound enlisted the support of her Californian cousin Jasmine to support the Big Red. Displaying fabulous team spirit with their matching Nebraska scarves, they warmed up for the game by tussling in a lively red-white scrimmage that was only halted when my wife intervened with dog treats.

The atmosphere at Player's Sports Grill was similarly spirited as we joined a group of Californians for Nebraska to watch the game. I could not help but feel sorry for the sole Hawkeyes fan in attendance who sat gamely at a table on his own amidst the sea of red. I managed to meet many of the Big Red fans, including one gentleman originally from Beatrice who reported that he misses the changes of season from his home town, including the winter. He and my wife are not quite on the same page with that sentiment, to put it mildly.

While she has fond memories of Fall and Spring in Omaha, she has no desire to endure another Winter on the prairie with its accompanying boots, gloves, scarves and flat car batteries.

After the game began, Iowa scored first and their lone supporter cheered bravely in the midst of the deafening silence from the red-clad crowd. I regret not having taken the opportunity to talk with this brave soul who was carrying the flag for his alma mater in the hinterlands of Orange County, California, before he left before the end of the second quarter. I would have liked to hear his perspective on the many years of

cross-border rivalry and also congratulate him on his pluck in wading into a sea of red to support his beloved Hawkeyes.

As usual the Nebraska crowd was very good-natured while they supported their boys. Dirk's humorous comments provided much entertainment on one side of the room, with my favorite comment of his arriving after a muffed punt return by the "Iowegians" as he called them. "I love a good muff!" he cried, much to the amusement of certain sections of the crowd. However one young man in his late 20s seemed to take the whole game very seriously, and was not shy to express his opinions out loud for all to hear as he coached the game from the sidelines. It seemed that he was also a conspiracy theorist because after a couple of questionable penalties called against Nebraska he pronounced "They" (presumably the referees or those who give the referees their marching orders) "have a vested interest in keeping Iowa undefeated!" I did agree with his opinion on a later coaching decision when halfway through the 4th quarter with the Huskers down 17-28 and the ball on the Iowa 19-yard line, the play call was to pass instead of kicking a field goal on 4th and 1. Unfortunately for the Huskers and for all of us in attendance at the bar, the pass fell incomplete and the young man talked loudly about it all the way through the subsequent commercial break, the next Iowa possession which was a three-and-out, and the Iowa timeout in between.

For better or worse, the game itself was in many ways a microcosm of the Huskers' season. Flashes of brilliance were interspersed with penalties that should have been avoided and errant passes that either fell incomplete or were intercepted. The one source of stability amidst the maelstrom was the generally solid performance of the Blackshirts defense. The undefeated Iowegians (I love that term) were held to three-and-out in several critical situations that gave the ball back to the offense with the opportunity to stay in the game. Just as they have done all year, the Nebraska players never gave up and fought hard throughout, but in the end 8 penalties for 95 yards and 4 interceptions were too much to overcome and the game was lost by a mere 8 points.

The regular season thus ends with a 5-7 record, but it is worth remembering that most of those lost games went down to the final play of the game and the average losing margin throughout the seven losses was a mere 4.4 points. But for some bad luck in some crucial situations, the Big Red could have easily won 7 or 8 games.

While this was not the season that most Nebraska fans hoped for, there is much to look forward to for next year. Lily and Jasmine are already in training to provide dogged and loyal support.

CHAPTER THIRTEEN

MY BOWL RUNNETH OVER

Nebraska has never played in a bowl game after winning only 5 games during the regular season, but according to my research the Huskers once went to a bowl game after winning 6 games. This took place in 1954, during which the Huskers' regular season record was 6-5. On January 1, 1955 the Huskers lost to Duke in the Orange Bowl by a score of 34-7 in front of 68,750 spectators, having trailed only 14-7 early in the 3rd quarter.

Big Red fans in 2015 are all too well aware of the fact that the team is bringing a 5-7 record to the battle against UCLA in the Foster Farms Bowl on December 26th of this year. However some creative thinking was called for on the part of the NCAA as there were a total of 40 bowl games to be filled for 2015, and three too few

NU	NEBRASKA FOOTBALL	OPP.
28	BRIGHAM YOUNG	33
48	S. ALABAMA	9
33	MIAMI	36
36	SOUTHERN MISS	29
13	ILLINOIS	14
21	WISCONSIN	23
48	MINNESOTA	25
28	NORTHWESTERN	30
45	PURDUE	55
39	MICHIGAN STATE	38
31	RUTGERS	14
20	IOWA	28

teams with at least 6 wins on their résumé at the end of the regular season to fill the 80 available spaces.

There were many football-related criteria that could have been used to select three teams to fill the empty spots in the lineup from among those who had only won 5 games, such as the lowest average losing margin or the most points scored, but to their credit the organizers chose to use a measurement unrelated to athletic activities. In a refreshing return to the *raison d'être* of universities everywhere, the Academic Progress Rating (APR) was used to determine which of the 5-7 teams around the country would be offered a bowl invitation.

The APR is a term-by-term measure of eligibility and retention for Division I student-athletes that was developed as an early indicator of eventual graduation rates. It was introduced as a result of concerns that the majority of student-athletes were not graduating with qualifications to prepare them for life beyond college.

While having letters after his name may not be a concern for the rare football player who goes on to a long-lived and successful career in the NFL, only a very small proportion of each year's senior class (less than 3%) ever make it to the ranks of the professionals. And then according to the NFL Players Association, the average career length of the talented few who make the cut is about 3.3 years. Having a meaningful college degree under their belt is therefore important to all but the Tom Bradys and Peyton Mannings of the world, and even then a debilitating injury early in their NFL careers

Thomas E. Brady Jr.
If you want to play with the big boys, you gotta learn how to play in the tall grass. Family I love you all. FB 1-4; BKB 1-2; BSB 1-4; BLOCK 4; JSA 2; TRIVIA 1-4; FRIAR 4

would have quickly returned them to the ranks of the merely mortal.

The most recent APR rates available for breaking the tie among the 5-7 teams were those from the 2013-14 academic year. Nebraska was top of the list with an APR of .985, followed by Missouri at .976, and Minnesota and San Jose State tied at .975. However for reasons of its own Missouri declined the bowl invitation, leaving the tied pair of schools to round out the remaining vacancies.

While I'm sure all Big Red fans were pleased that we would get to see the Huskers in action once more before the season close, I was personally pleased that the whole APR-based decision process had provided football fans across the country with a reminder of the prime reason that colleges even exist. Although football and other athletic programs were originally created to provide opportunities for students to gain exercise and a temporary diversion from the rigor of their studies, in many colleges across the country the pendulum has swung in the opposite direction.

Having worked at a private university myself, I know full well how difficult it can be to obtain funding for a school's academic facilities and staff. I've seen the same problems at state schools as they compete for precious government funds and so I can certainly understand the temptation to develop a successful football program that brings in significant revenue from fans, boosters and television rights. Another substantial benefit I have witnessed from successful football programs is that they lead to the establishment of a large and loyal alumni base that remains connected to the school, providing yet another source of fundraising.

Like so many things in life, a balanced approach is the key to avoiding the three-part Catch-22 that comes with a successful football program:

1. "We can't attract quality students because we don't have enough money to build strong academic programs."

2. "We can't use our football program to raise money for the academic programs until we have enough students to raise money to build the football program."

3. "If we create a successful football program, we won't attract quality students because they will regard us as a football school and not an academic school."

To put it in other words, if all of the money raised through the football program is used to improve and build the football program, the academic side suffers and eventually causes a shift in the school's focus to football. This in turn reduces the perceived value of degrees earned at the school and encourages serious academic students to choose other locations for their studies. It seems to me that the two most balanced schools I have seen during my travels this season with the Huskers are Nebraska which leads the nation with 320 Academic All-Americans within the athletic department, and Rutgers with its strong academic reputation.

But speaking of balance (and stepping off my soapbox), the challenge for Husker fans would be to pace themselves through their Christmas celebrations and visits with distant relatives so that their calendars and minds would be clear on

December 26th to cheer their Huskers to a sound and redemptive 6th victory of the year.

Even though the Bowl season would officially get underway with the New Mexico Bowl, quickly followed by four others with captivating titles such as the Camellia Bowl and the New Mexico Bowl, the attention of Nebraska fans everywhere would be focused on the NCAA National Women's Volleyball title match between the Huskers and the Texas Longhorns.

The Huskers won the right to go to the final by beating Kansas in a semi-final played at the CenturyLink Center in Omaha, while also setting an NCAA attendance record of 17,551.

The two finalists were evenly-matched and any football fans who managed to tear themselves away from the delights of watching Georgia State take on San Jose State in the Cure Bowl to watch the "Volley Bowl" instead, would be in for an exciting match in front of a very lively and enthusiastic crowd.

Speaking of Bowl games, one Husker football player who would not make the trip to San Francisco was Jonathan Rose, who was dismissed from the team after yet another violation of team rules. As a result the team would be without the services of the Senior Cornerback who appeared in nine games this season and was suspended for three others. Most importantly however, the dismissal of Rose sent a strong signal to the other players on the roster that there would always be consequences for the violation of team rules. In the long run, the consistent enforcement of this type of discipline helps to not only shape the character of the players but also bind them closer together as a unit. Kudos to Mike Riley and his staff for not only setting the boundaries but also staying the course and enforcing the rules.

With so many Bowl games scheduled in December, it was difficult for us couch-based players to keep up with the schedule. Take the first set of games, for example. The New Orleans bowl, New Mexico Bowl and Las Vegas Bowl would all be played on the same day - but where? How were we supposed to tell from those very imaginative names where each game would take place? I figured that the Camellia Bowl would be played in a flourishing Botanical Garden somewhere in the south, and the Cure Bowl would be played in the grounds of St. Jude's Children's Hospital, but trying to figure out those other three was just too confusing.

The Foster Farms Bowl on the other hand was much less troublesome, if you would allow me to explain its background. In my self-appointed capacity as the Australian Cultural Ambassador to Nebraska, a large part of my job is to dispel the numerous myths and misconceptions held by many mid-Westerners about the mysterious Land Down Under.

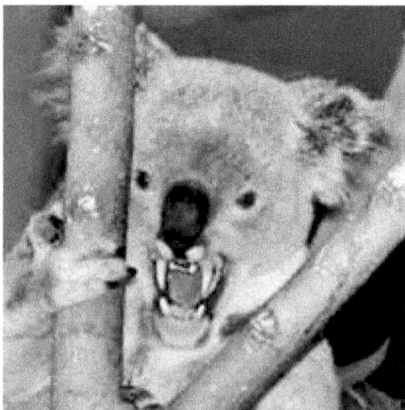

While of course it can't be denied that the country's wildlife population includes various poisonous snakes, spiders and other lurking creatures such as the vampire-like Drop Bears who spend most of their waking time conspiring to prey on unsuspecting tourists by leaping from the trees and satisfying their thirst for blood, there are many other very positive aspects of the land that are less well known outside Australia. (For safety's sake all visitors to the country are advised to keep their eyes on the foliage above them to help avert the threat of a sudden Drop Bear attack. And by the way for those who may be worried about being attacked by a crocodile while swimming in the tropical waters in the north of the country, in many cases there is no cause for concern because the sharks have eaten most of the crocodiles.)

To continue in this positive and uplifting vein, I can assure you that one of the things you may have heard about and treated with some skepticism is in reality quite true - beer really does grow on trees in Australia. In fact one of the larger agribrewcultural operators in Australia is the sponsor of Nebraska's Bowl game. I know that many people have been wondering about the origin of the name for the Foster Farms Bowl, and now you have the answer complete with compelling photographic evidence. You're welcome.

Another lesser-known fact is that one of the major sports played Down Under is Australian Rules football. This game is played by two teams of 18 men on an oval-shaped field 200 yards long, and the continuous action takes place over four

30-minute quarters. This may sound like a tall tale but unlike American football, in Aussie Rules every player is lean, extremely fit and kicks the ball numerous times throughout the game.

Meanwhile, a few days before the Foster Farms Bowl the lean and fit Nebraska Women's Volleyball team beat Texas in straight sets to win the national championship, setting yet another attendance record in the process. It was inspiring to watch the game on national TV and hear the enthusiastic support from the Omaha crowd. Their raucous shouts of GO BIG RED! would undoubtedly be echoed at the Foster Farms Bowl with the fans hoping that the Husker lads would echo the results of their co-ed counterparts.

But before the game could commence, there was some serious tailgating to be done.

It was around this same time of year in the late 90s that I first heard the term "tailgating" in connection with a football game. I was about to watch a game that had been promoted for weeks as crucial in deciding that year's national college champion team – it may have been the Rose Bowl, if memory serves me correctly. The pre-game telecast began with a helicopter's-eye view of the stadium and its surrounds, with thousands of cars already in the parking lot and thousands more on the nearby roads waiting their turn to enter. As I contemplated the bumper-to-bumper traffic and wondered what kind of devotion that would cause college fans to travel across the country and spend a public holiday stuck in traffic in an unfamiliar city, one of the commentators startled me from my reverie by noting "There has been a lot of tailgating going on all around the stadium for the past couple of days. It's such a great tradition for College Bowl games".

As a relative newcomer to North America at that time, and an even more recent follower of football who had only lately began to understand the basic rules of the game, the term "tailgating" simply meant driving one's car as close as possible to the car in front. The picture I was seeing on the screen with cars moving slowly in heavy traffic coincided perfectly with my understanding of the term, and so I was amazed to think that the dedicated fans had been stuck in heavy nose-to-tail traffic for a "couple of days" as they waited to get into the stadium grounds and find a parking space. Meanwhile the camera cut to several shots of fans picnicking from the back of their cars in the parking lot, and all I could do was sympathize with how hungry they must have been after being stuck in their cars and enduring traffic that was not only heavy but also stressful as everyone tried to stay on the bumper in front of them. It was little wonder that some of them were drinking beer after such an ordeal.

But before I could relax and feel relieved for the fans who had safely made it to the parking lot, the commentators upped the ante all over again when they said in a matter-of-fact way "Well of course enjoying your favorite beverage is always a big part of tailgating. Some fans like their bourbon while they tailgate and others have their beer of choice..." I was too stunned to hear what he said next – as if the sheer volume of traffic going to the game were not enough, the drivers all tailgate one another and make a point of drinking while they're doing it! It was at this point that I decided I would never go to a college Bowl game. No sir, watching it on TV would be just fine thank you very much.

However as the years went by and I learned the difference between a touchdown and a touchback, I also learned that "tailgating" had another meaning in addition to the one I had grown up with. Nevertheless I had yet to experience going to a Bowl game, much less the hospitable type of tailgating that goes with it. For that reason, combined with the self-sacrificing principles of journalistic integrity, I made the decision to not only attend the Foster Farms Bowl but also to sign up for the "Official Tailgate Party" that would take place at the stadium starting 3 hours before the game.

Given that the sponsor's fine product would likely be flowing in abundance, I was sure this party would give me lots of opportunity to meet my fellow Nebraska fans and learn more about the long-standing tradition of tailgating. But just to be on the safe side I planned to take an Uber car to the game and avoid the tailgating traffic on the roads!

I arrived at San Francisco airport just before 9am on the day after Christmas expecting to see the usual sea of red shirts prior to a Huskers game. I guess I had been spoiled by red shirts surrounding me all season but I should have realized that there were at least two other airports located within 30 miles of the stadium where the game was to be played, not to mention the fact that there would be a lot of people who had reasons to travel to SanFran that had nothing to do with Nebraska's Bowl game. (The poor misguided fools were probably on their way to visit friends and family at their homes instead of packing up the whole group and doing their visiting at the Foster Farms Bowl). In any case, I only saw one red shirt that morning at the airport and was forced to remind myself that I was not in Lincoln anymore.

"Folks in Nebraska are not expecting a lot from this game today, but I'm just glad to get out of the snow in Omaha." This was the less than enthusiastic comment from the man I met in the rental car line, but rather than let his words erode my wildly-optimistic confidence about the Huskers' prospects against UCLA, I put his glass-half-empty outlook down to the fact that he had spent the last 24 hours surrounded by frigid weather and 10 inches of snow (and perhaps also some out-of-town relatives that he would rather not be surrounded by).

Just as I had planned to do, in the middle of the afternoon I arrived at Levi's Stadium by Uber car. The parking lot near the stadium was already half-full with groups of fans from both teams enjoying themselves with their favorite beverages while smoke from their various cooking operations curled into the air. The red groups seemed to slightly outnumber the blue, but all seemed to be enjoying the sunny day in good spirits despite the 54 degree temperature and a wind that made it seem colder. The gate attendant would not allow the Uber car to enter the parking lot and thus I had to walk

INCREDIBOWL

FOSTER FARMS

BOWL

SATURDAY · DEC 26
6:15 PM · LEVI'S STADIUM
SFBowl.org
yp

across to where he told me I would find the "Official Pre-Game Tailgate Party". Unfortunately the attendant sent me to the wrong place, and I had to seek directions from another employee. Sad to say this disastrous mix-up caused me to lose some 15 precious minutes of ~~drinking time~~ quality journalistic research time while I found my way to the party.

This was to be the first organized tailgate event that I had ever attended, and I had imagined that the crowd at such a gathering would be a mixture of colors as fans mingled with one another and talked about the game. However once inside the Great America Pavilion I quickly found that the large hall contained some 400 people who had self-segregated into red shirts at one end of the building and blue at the other. There were a number of food stations set up around the large rooms, serving a wide range of choices including chicken wings, BBQ beef and pork, tortillas, and hot dogs. Everyone seemed to be in a good mood while they enjoyed themselves, and so I quickly forgot about my Kumbaya expectations of inter-collegial brotherhood and set myself to the important task of looking for the Foster's.

Amazing as it may sound, there was no Foster's being served anywhere in the building! Initially I was shocked but then I realized that the sponsors must be saving their precious imported nectar for that magical moment after the game when the winners traditionally crack bottles of champagne – but instead they will crack bottles of Foster's. What a stroke of marketing genius! I would never have thought of that idea – I guess that's why those PR guys fly in helicopters while I scuttle around town in a little Kia.

But all was not lost, despite the absence of Foster's. I soon spotted a booth advertising Stella Artois, which I do regard to be an acceptable substitute for Australian beer in an emergency such as this. I happily crossed the floor in the Stella direction, already tasting in my mind the smooth lagery Belgian bubbles, yet I was blissfully unaware of the cruel twist of fate that awaited me. In a classic bait-and-switch manoeuver, the booth that so boldly advertised Stella Artois was in fact serving <gasp> only Bud and Bud Light. Yes dear reader, I know you're shocked and I can still hardly believe it myself, but the pictures tell the heartbreaking story of the cruel deception played on a poor innocent abroad.

It was all I could do to stop myself from sinking to my knees and crying out the immortal final line of Tennessee Williams' famous play "Cat on a Hot Tin Roof".

"STELLA!" I wanted to cry out in anguish.

"We agree with you. We're about to switch to wine" said Gary. He too had noted the absence of both Foster's and Stella Artois from the pre-game tailgate party, and sympathized with my plight. I had earlier spoken with an ex-Nebraskan living in Montana who told me that he thought that the sponsor of the Foster Farms Bowl had something to do with chicken and not beer. Of course I didn't believe him – I think all that cold weather in Montana must have formed icicles upstairs for the poor guy. Everyone knows that farms have chickens, and naturally a farm where the beer grows on trees would probably also have a few chickens.

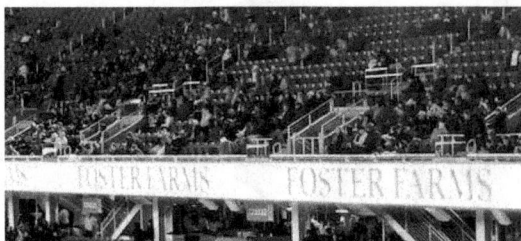

Even though Gary seemed to make sense on the surface, I was a bit perturbed by the details of his background. It seems he was born in Iowa, studied law at Mizzou and then lived 30 years in San Francisco before moving to the Sonoma Valley 14 years ago. His saving graces are that he married a lovely lady from Broken Bow, NE and he is a Big Red fan. I would imagine that when his wife's parents first heard about Gary from their daughter, they were so pleased to hear that he was a Husker fan that they were able to forgive him for being a lawyer.

Gary's wife's parents were both students in Lincoln in the 1940s but had not met one another until they both traveled to watch Nebraska play in the Rose Bowl on New Year's Day in 1941. As mentioned in an earlier chapter, there had been much excitement about Nebraska's first-ever post-season game and Gary's future father-in-law drove some 1,300 hundred miles to California with a group of friends while the lady who later became his mother-in-law traveled alone by train. Even though the Huskers lost that particular game, it was obviously a memorable experience for many other reasons!

As I moved around the room and met Anthony I figured I would also see him during the game on the big screen. He is originally from Page, NE but now lives in Lincoln, CA where he is currently stationed in the Air Force. He tries to watch every Husker game at a local watch site but his rule-of-thumb is to drive to any live Nebraska game within 8 hours of where he is living or visiting.

Anthony has found during his travels, just as my wife and I have done, that there are Husker fan clubs all over the country and in many overseas locations.

No-one could doubt Anthony's devotion to the Big Red but I didn't have the heart to ask if he dresses the same way for televised games as he does for the games he watches in person.

I also met another active duty serviceman at the party. I didn't catch the name of Steve's Nebraska home town but he told me he now works in the Mojave Desert with the US Navy. I didn't ask him about the name of his ship because I was too busy trying to recall from my high school geography class the name of the ocean that borders that part of California. The Mirage Sea perhaps?

But before I could make further sense of the conversation, we were interrupted by a line of shiny gold tubas that snaked its way into the building and made its way to the segregated blue end of the room, followed by drums and a flurry of cheerleaders. We soon realized that a section of the UCLA band had taken a wrong turn while making their way to the stadium. But before we could point out the error of their ways, the cheerleaders had formed a couple of pyramids and were throwing scantily-clad girls in the air and catching them again before they landed on the dessert table.

Turning back to the red end of the room it wasn't long until I was joined in conversation by an extended family group. "2001" they said almost in unison, the father and son. I had asked the red-clad pair about their favorite memory of Nebraska football. They went on to explain a road trip they had made from their home in Reno, NV to watch the pivotal game of that 2001 season when the two top teams in the country clashed in Lincoln: Nebraska vs Oklahoma. The visitors were riding a 20-game winning streak and the Huskers entered the game at 8-0. Pat, who had been born and raised in Omaha had spontaneously decided that his son Pat Jr, aged 13 at that time, needed to see for himself the Big Red spectacle that he had heard so much about. And what an exciting game it promised to be, with potential implications for the national championship.

The main problem was that in October 2001, airline schedules were not yet back to normal following 9/11 and so it was impossible to find a pair of plane tickets for the 1,200 mile journey. The other problem was that Pat had no tickets for the game. But with the spirit of resourcefulness that seems to flow abundantly in the veins of those of Nebraskan stock, the two simply jumped in the car and set off for a 22-hour journey across the country. With no tickets for the game.

After arriving at the stadium early on the day of the game, with some difficulty Pat was eventually able to obtain tickets for himself and his son whom I imagine by that time was very excited to see Eric Crouch and his team. The game was a hard-fought affair but the crucial play came towards the end of the 4th quarter when Crouch sealed the 20-10 win by scoring a touchdown on a trick play pass from the aptly-named freshman Mike Stuntz. I could see it in their eyes and hear it in their voices that both men regarded that weekend trip as the ultimate father-son experience.

And now 15 years later, another family event was taking place as Pat and his family had driven to the bowl game from Reno while Pat's brother and family had flown in from Omaha. Their wives Pam and Karen had come well-prepared for the event with their Nebraska accessories as well as ample coats and blankets for the family to protect against the cold weather predicted for the game. The two ladies admitted they are not big fans of watching football in the cold, and confessed that they had bailed out of the Iowa game during the half-time break and watched the second half in front of a large screen in a comfortably warm Lincoln bar.

It was at that moment that I realized the UCLA band had not been lost at all – they were simply looking for a warm place to go before the game started. It's just a pity there was no Foster's on hand to warm them up!

After reluctantly leaving the warm surrounds of the indoor tailgate party I made my way over to Levi's Stadium for the Foster Farms Bowl where the Huskers would take on the heavily-favored Bruins. UCLA fans dressed in blue mixed good-naturedly with the red-clad Nebraska fans as they entered the modern stadium that had been built just a year or two ago for the San Francisco 49ers, but once inside each group went its separate way. The segregation I had witnessed at the pre-game tailgate party carried through to the game itself as it seemed that the west side of the stadium had been reserved for Bruins fans and the east side for Husker fans.

In many ways we could have been almost anywhere in America except for one thing. Just when I was getting over the traumatic experience of the Great Stella Artois Deception, not to mention the as-yet-unseen Foster's beer, I was thrown into a tailspin all over again by the indignities perpetrated on that great staple of cold weather football games, the hot dog. Ok, I was willing to accept that there would be no Valentino's in the stands, nor Runza's, but vegan hot dogs for crying out loud? I mean, who ever heard of a vegan hot dog? And where else but in California could you find one? Where I grew up the slang term for a dachshund was a "sausage dog". In Canada and the US they call them a "wiener dog". But what on earth do they call a dachshund in California – a "zucchini dog"? And what kind of garnishings do you use on a vegan hot dog – sautéed lentils and quinoa dressing? They'd never get away with such tomfoolery in Lincoln!

After a shock like that it was only the presence of more sane and sensible sights such as grown men wearing giant plastic corn cobs and Santa hats on their heads that allowed me to calm down so that I could focus on the game. The stadium looked less than half full with 33,527 fans in attendance, but their enthusiastic support combined with the presence of bands from both teams served to create a festive atmosphere despite the falling temperatures. Apparently the designers of the stadium had forgotten the small detail of adding a roof to their giant sporting shrine, but many fans had come well-prepared to face the conditions.

For example the four members of the family in front of me were each wearing several layers of clothing underneath the blankets that covered them. The husband is originally from Omaha and has lived in Sacramento for the past 30 years, but it was good to see that he was doing his best to raise his two teenage daughters in the Husker faith.

The game began well for the Bruins. On the first possession of the game they scored a touchdown within the space of 4 minutes as they marched 80 yards down the field looking like a well-oiled machine. Less than 7 minutes later the Huskers returned the favor by covering 75 yards to score a touchdown on their own first possession of the game. The key difference between these two drives was that UCLA's approach was focused on passing plays whereas Nebraska's was focused on rushing by three different players, most notably Cross and Ozigbo.

I was encouraged to see that the Big Red had established so early in the game that several different players had the capacity to run the ball against the Bruins defense. However my excitement was tempered when the Bruins scored the next two touchdowns, making it look very easy as they did so. By midway through the second quarter the Bruins led 21-7. But the Huskers refused to back down and continued their run-heavy offense based around several players including Armstrong. Some long pass completions at critical moments combined with solid rushing saw the Huskers score two touchdowns of their own to level the scores one minute before halftime. The Huskers were looking good and we really had a game on our hands going into the second half!

Since this was to be the last game of the season, it was also my last chance to conduct my own unscientific survey to determine the approximate percentage of Husker fans who know the words to the team's fight song "Dear Old Nebraska U". I was seated within earshot of the band, and after each Husker touchdown I followed the traditions I had observed in Lincoln as the music got underway: the waving arms...the rhythmic clapping...and then the song. I would sing both verses of the song at the top of my lungs, followed by the three shouts of "Go Huskers!" at the appropriate moments cued by the band. This was in turn followed by repeating the two verses of the song, and the grand finale was four shouts of "Go Big Red!" Of course I knew that all the people around me would surely join in participating in most of these traditions, but my aim was to see how many would sing along to the song with me.

After going through this routine for several Husker touchdowns, I must say I had never felt so lonely in my life. I could see some other red sections of the crowd enjoying their own celebrations of these same traditions that my wife had followed as a student at UNL in late 70s, but an air of bemused silence reigned in my part of the stadium. While making a spectacle of myself I had learned nothing about whether any of my fellow Husker fans knew the words to the song, but I did learn that they were a tolerant bunch who were polite enough to put up with the antics of a lunatic foreigner in their midst without calling Security to have him escorted to the exits. However I was later relieved to a certain extent when Anthony from the tailgate party suddenly appeared on the big screen at the other end of the field, complete with his red-and-white face paint and corn hat. I bet *he* would have sung along with me.

On the field the second half continued in the same way that it had begun. The Huskers dominated the game with their run-by-committee approach and continued to wear down the Bruins' defense, while the Huskers defense was all but impenetrable. By 38 seconds into the 4th quarter the score was 37-21 and the Huskers had scored 30 unanswered points. The Blackshirts had completely shut down the well-oiled Bruins offense that had so quickly put three touchdowns on the board in the first half.

And then just as quickly as it had disappeared, the machine-like UCLA blitzkrieg offense suddenly reappeared.

Within the space of 3 minutes, the Bruins marched 76 yards down the field with 8 plays to score a touchdown followed by a silky-smooth 2-point conversion to make the score 29-37. When Nebraska's next drive stalled, the Bruins got the ball back on their own 27-yard line with nine minutes left to play. After watching the way the Bruins had run their last drive I was seriously concerned that they would march down and score another 8 points to tie the game. My worst fears looked like coming to fruition as the Bruins used 5 plays to reach the Nebraska 17-yard line. This next series of plays would be critical to the result of the game.

On first down the UCLA quarterback Rosen threw a rare incomplete pass. On second down his receiver dropped a pass he would normally have caught. On third down the Black-shirts broke through the Bruins offensive line and sacked Rosen for the loss of 11 yards. And on fourth down UCLA's 46-yard field goal attempt missed wide left. But all was not lost for UCLA, and they would have another possession fol-lowing a Huskers three-and-out. With just under 5 minutes left in the game they got the ball back on their own 46-yard line. Five plays later they were on the Husker 32 with a first down. However once again the Blackshirts stood firm and intercepted Rosen's fourth down pass one yard from the end zone.

With 3:08 remaining, the Huskers needed to run out the clock starting from their own 1-yard line. This was no easy proposition given the poor field position and the fact that UCLA still had two timeouts left. Nevertheless the Huskers were up to the challenge and continued to run the ball against the tiring Bruins defense, with Armstrong and Carter making key runs to reach first downs at important moments when they were most needed to seal the game.

It was a remarkable victory that will live long in the memories of the players and fans. Even more remarkable was that we saw Mike Riley in an animated and excited state after the game. "How 'bout those Huskers!" were his first words into the microphone in the center of the field at the trophy presentation ceremony. I'm pretty sure that if you study the photo carefully you'll see they've got some celebratory Foster's out there on the field!

After living through the many twists and turns of the 2015 season and witnessing face-to-face the reactions of Coach Riley and his key players after some heartbreaking losses, in my mind the exciting and hard-fought 37-29 win over UCLA in the Foster Farms Bowl could be summed up in just three words.

Vindication. Redemption. Satisfaction.

First of all, the game represented vindication for Riley and his coaches as it demonstrated that their calm and unruffled approach to managing their team can be successful in the long term. I could see the hurt in Riley's eyes at the post-game press conferences following close losses at home against Wisconsin and Northwestern, and as the season went on I could sense the growing frustration among the reporters and journalists around me but Riley always maintained his composure and repeated what almost became a mantra: "It was disappointing to lose today but we coaches need to identify what went wrong and then fix it. They're a great bunch of kids who respond to coaching and we'll get back to work on Monday and move forward from there." Meanwhile a minority of fans that I met regarded this kind of even-keeled "Mister Rogers" approach, as they termed it, to be a sign that Riley was not committed to Nebraska and didn't care whether the team won or lost. These reactive fans obviously prefer a reactive coaching style, but anyone who has ever played a team sport under a reactive and punitive coach would know that while this type of approach may work in the short term, it is not a recipe for building a successful program over the long term. And while accepting the trophy after the game, Riley emphasized his long-term view and pointed the way forward to next year for his exuberant group of players. I hope that message was also understood by the thousands of Big Red fans at the stadium and watching on TV.

For the Nebraska players the game represented redemption for the tumultuous season they had endured. While on paper a 6-7 record is nothing to write home about, the final game proved to the players and fans that this team was much stronger than its record suggested. Several games that were lost by narrow margins in the last minute could easily have been victories, and I applaud Coach Riley for his public refusal to blame bad luck in those losses. It would have been easy to allow the players to take on a victim-like approach and blame others for those losses, but instead he encouraged his team to take a positive forward-looking approach and focus on controlling the aspects of the game that were in their power to control. For Tommy Armstrong in particular, his almost flawless display at quarterback with 174 passing yards, 76 rushing yards and two touchdowns was redemption for some earlier games in which his decision-making had been criticized in some quarters. Winning the award for Offensive Player of the Game must have felt sweet indeed, but in his typical humble style Armstrong deflected the praise towards his teammates and coaches.

For the ever-loyal Nebraska fans, the underdog Huskers' win over the 8-4 Bruins created a very satisfying note on which to end the season. The game had something to please fans of every persuasion: it was a complete team effort with 62 rushes by 9 different players; 12 completed passes to 7 different receivers; and an outstanding performance by the defense that captured two interceptions and allowed the UCLA offense less than 22 minutes of playing time for the game. That effort, combined with some other good performances during the season that fell just short of victory, should serve to satisfy and resolve the fears of any doubters who thought the Riley experiment was doomed to failure and that the victory over Michigan State was a fluke.

The Huskers are back on track, baby! Bring on 2016!

EPILOGUE

NO PLACE LIKE NEBRASKA

"Well, you sure picked a bad year for it" he said, sympathetically. This was a sentiment I heard expressed many times by Husker fans when I described my ongoing project to follow the team throughout the season and travel far and wide to meet as many fans as possible. On one level they were right, of course. The season began with a very close loss and at no point did the Huskers' win-loss record surpass the .500 mark. But the performance of the team on the field was only a part of the reason I spent some 14 weeks driving and flying across the country to follow the 2015 football season. I also wanted to learn about the devoted and loyal Nebraskans who support and follow their boys through thick and thin, from the pre-season scrimmage game at a packed stadium through to the Bowl game that puts a capstone on the season.

The up-and-down season that turned out to be Nebraska's third losing season since 1962 provided ample opportunity for me to witness the reactions of fans young and old as their loyalty was tested by the unusually poor results. It was not a difficult matter to strike up a conversation under circumstances such as these, because almost everyone had an opinion about the changes or improvements needed to bring the team back to its winning ways.

During a typical winning season the discussion would center around the margin of victory in a given game rather than play calling or whether a certain running back or receiver should be used more frequently. For example my father-in-law Tom loved his Huskers dearly and had been very accustomed to seeing them rack up winning seasons throughout his adult life. However I was never able to discuss the different aspects of the game with him because he had never had to think about it before.

The team had won consistently throughout Tom's memory and there was no need to question how or why because the results on the scoreboard spoke for themselves. I recall talking with him during the period where Bill Callahan was coaching and the team was losing more games than normal. His explanation was simple: if the team won a game it was because they had played what he called "Nebraska football" a losing game was explained by the fact that the team had *not* played "Nebraska football".

The roller-coaster ride that was the 2015 season caused fans all over Nebraska and elsewhere to focus more on the various elements of the football program such as the player composition, coaching and conditioning that affect the team's results on the field. This in turn gave me the opportunity to join in those fan discussions and gain further insight into "The Greatest Fans in College Football", as the gates at Memorial Stadium so proudly proclaim.

In that sense, I had picked a very good year to follow the Huskers.

Mike Riley had arrived during the off-season to take over the reins as Head Coach, and he would be the first to admit that it had not been an easy year. Apart from his extensive football résumé he impressed me with his calm exterior and his declaration that he regarded the development of the character of his players to be an important part of his role. Although some may have initially misinterpreted Riley's soft-spoken, even demeanor as an indication that he would be soft on his players, a series of suspensions of various players throughout the season for the violation of team rules served to demonstrate that he said what he meant and meant what he said.

Lest anyone need reminding of the tenuousness of the position as Head Coach at major colleges, the 2015 provided a couple of clear examples right under the noses of Husker fans. The campaign to fire Miami coach Al Golden that was so publicly conducted by banner-flying planes eventually came to fruition in October after a 58-0 home loss to Clemson. Miami had entered the game as 7-point underdogs and some had even expected an upset by the Hurricanes. Golden was fired the next day with his team at 4-3, but in retrospect it might have been a little harsh to fire him for a loss against a team that almost won the national championship two months later.

Meanwhile the Rutgers coach Kyle Flood whom the fans had booed so publicly during the Nebraska game was eventually fired after the last game of the season. He had earlier suspended for three games for violating a university compliance policy and seven of his players had been arrested during the year on various charges. To put it mildly, I would imagine that this is not the atmosphere into which a responsible parent would want to entrust their son for four years of his young life!

Rutgers had finished their regular season at 4-8, compared to the Huskers 5-6 which meant neither team qualified for a post-season Bowl game. However Nebraska and two other teams were invited to Bowl games as there were not enough teams with a minimum 6-6 record to fill the available spaces in the 40 games. A debate raged in many circles about the greedy commercialism of the Bowl sponsors who had provided funds to create new games where none had previously existed, and how inviting teams with worse than 6-6 records demeaned the value of the Bowl season as a whole. I could see the point of these arguments but I thought the commentators who urged a boycott of the games played by 5-6 teams were taking it a bit too far. Especially when all three 5-6 teams ended up winning their games!

From a football point of view we had learned that a team's win-loss record is not a reliable indicator of the strength of that team. This was especially the case for the Huskers who had suffered so many close losses during the season. Even the undefeated Michigan State Head Coach had been very wary of taking on the Huskers as he regarded them as a much better team than their 3-6 record at that time suggested.

Nevertheless the Huskers had finished their season at 6-7 and of course everyone wanted to know why there were so many losses. Fingers were pointed at the penalties that had plagued the Huskers throughout the season, and there was much debate among fans about the proportion of running plays compared to passing. After a review of those statistics from the 2015 season I came up with a few findings of my own.

Penalties

- In games that they won, the Huskers averaged 5.7 penalties.
- In games that they lost, the Huskers averaged 8.6 penalties.
- The worst case was 12 penalties for 98 yards. This happened twice – once in a winning game and once in a losing game.

Run vs. Pass

- In games that they won, the Huskers averaged 1.6 run attempts for every pass attempt.
- In games that they lost, the Huskers averaged 0.9 run attempts for every pass attempt.
- The highest Run-Pass Attempt Ratio for the year was 3.3 which occurred in the Bowl game (62 rushes and 19 pass attempts).
- The lowest Run-Pass Attempt Ratio for the year was 0.6 which occurred in the Purdue game (29 rushes and 48 pass attempts).
- In all 7 losing games, Run-Pass Attempt Ratio only exceeded 1.0 twice.
- In all 5 winning games, Run-Pass Attempt Ratio was never below 1.0.

Conclusions

Two (admittedly unscientific) conclusions can be drawn from this brief analysis:

- Penalties did not have a significant effect on the team's results.
- The team did significantly better when it favored running plays over passing plays.

I'll leave it to much smarter football brains than mine to decide what all of this means for Tommy Armstrong's senior season in 2016.

However coming back to 2015, football was only a part of the journey that I had set out to undertake. I also wanted to understand why Nebraskans are so proud of their State and so fiercely loyal to their Huskers. The beginnings of the answers to these questions started to seep into my consciousness as soon as I ventured outside Omaha and Lincoln where I had always spent the most time on earlier visits.

Driving to places like Kearney, Beatrice, Aurora and Nebraska City allowed me to not only admire the beautiful countryside with its gently rolling hills covered like a blanket with neat rows of corn, but also to meet the hard-working, down-to-earth, open-hearted people who call Nebraska home and would give you the shirt off their back. Despite the cold winters and the isolation that sometimes comes with living in smaller communities, from no-one that I met in Nebraska did I ever gain a sense that they would rather live elsewhere if they could. As I have learned through my travels around the country, there are large numbers of native-born Nebraskans who do indeed choose to live elsewhere but they share very similar characteristics to their compatriots who still reside within the borders of the Cornhusker State.

No matter where I traveled during the writing of this book, I received a warm and genuine welcome. From the VFW in Beatrice, to the tailgate parties in Lincoln, to the sports bars in Oklahoma, Texas and California I was treated with the type of kindness and sincere honesty that restores faith in one's fellow man.

From the moment my Indian-born friend Vinay arrived in Kearney to start his new job he was welcomed and made to feel a part of the family of employees where he worked. He enjoyed his work and his colleagues during the five years that he lived there before moving to Seattle to take up an important position with a large international retail chain. I was fortunate to be at his farewell where I could see that both he and his co-workers were genuinely emotional about his departure.

But what is it that makes Nebraskans this way? Why do they take a man at his word and welcome strangers into their midst?

I believe I found the answers to those questions in Hooper when I researched my wife's family tree. Thousands upon thousands of settlers made their way across the plains to Nebraska during the homesteading days and found nothing but empty prairie bisected by a railway line. These brave souls such as my wife's great-great-grandparents had to bring everything they needed with them on their ox- and horse-drawn wagons. Digging up sod on the prairie to build an earthen home was only the beginning of the process of establishing themselves and making a life for their families. Working together as a family and working co-operatively with other families to build small communities were critical to their survival and mutual security against the elements. Under conditions such as these, people had to be able to rely on their neighbors as well as on themselves.

As new families arrived, it was important to welcome and assimilate the newcomers in order that growth could continue and enhance the benefits offered by the community for the common good. When illness struck or crops failed, the community could in many ways provide a safety net until the temporary crisis was over. Those families who had offered support to their peers during such situations could rest assured that their kindnesses would be reciprocated if the tables were turned. In due course as these small communities grew, churches and schools would be established to serve the local population.

Scenes such as this were repeated all over the state, with some differences related to those fortunate enough to have trees at hand for the building of their first homestead dwelling. Nevertheless it is my observation that same spirit of self-reliance and willingness to work hard and respect your fellow man that enabled the Nebraska Territory to grow from nothing to the self-sufficient 37th State of the Union has been passed through the generations and still lives on today.

It's no surprise therefore, that Nebraskans are proud of their state. And they have every right to be proud – after all, it was built by them and their forebears.

This leads us to the question of why Nebraskans are so proud of their university's football team. There are, I believe, two main reasons. The first relates to the long history of the institution whose name the team bears. The University of Nebraska was chartered by the legislature in 1869, during the homesteading period, and the school's football program began in 1890.

The second relates to the team's egalitarian "walk-on" program that allows any student at the school to try out for the football team. This allows players from rural areas who may never have been seen by a scout to make their case. The walk-ons who succeed in making the team are given the same access to training facilities and academic counseling as those players with scholarships. This program began in the early 1960s, and since that time 6 walk-ons have become All-American players and 29 have played in the NFL.

Together with the recruiting that is done within the state, this leads to the team's roster being composed largely of Nebraskans. For example the 2015-16 roster of 133 players included 59 Nebraskans from towns all over the state including Aurora, Beatrice and Kearney.

Putting these points together, in my opinion Nebraskans are proud of their team because it feels like they are part of it and it is part of them. The football program has been around longer than anyone living can remember, and almost everyone feels they have a connection to a past or present player that came from their town or high school, even if they have never actually met that player in person.

In summary, throughout the generations it was ordinary Nebraskans who built both their State and their football team. And Nebraskans today have every right to be proud of them both. It was a privilege to have felt like I was part of Nebraska in 2015.

There is no place like Nebraska,
Dear old Nebraska U.
Where the girls are the fairest,
The boys are the squarest,
Of any old school that I knew.

There is no place like Nebraska,
Where they're all true blue.
We'll all stick together,
In all kinds of weather,
For dear old Nebraska U.

Dear Old Nebraska U (There Is No Place Like Nebraska)
Words and Music by Harry Pecha, class of 1924

APPENDIX

SEASON RESULTS

Nebraska

Date	Opponent	Result	Standing
Sat 9/5	BYU	L 28 - 33	0-1
Sat 9/12	South Alabama	W 48 - 9	1-1
Sat 9/19	@ Miami (FL)	L 33 - 36	1-2
Sat 9/26	Southern Miss	W 36 - 28	2-2
Sat 10/3	@ Illinois	L 13 - 14	2-3
Sat 10/10	Wisconsin	L 21 - 23	2-4
Sat 10/17	@ Minnesota	W 48 - 25	3-4
Sat 10/24	Northwestern	L 28 - 30	3-5
Sat 10/31	@ Purdue	L 45 - 55	3-6
Sat 11/7	(7) Michigan St.	W 39 - 38	4-6
Sat 11/14	@ Rutgers	W 31 - 14	5-6
Fri 11/27	(4) Iowa	L 20 - 28	5-7
Sat 12/26	UCLA	W 37 - 29	6-7

Beatrice High School

Date	Opponent	Result	Standing
Fri 8/28	@ Skutt Catholic (Omaha, NE)	L 35 - 0	0-1
Fri 9/4	@ Ralston (Ralston, NE)	W 32 - 3	1-1
Fri 9/11	Elkhorn (Elkhorn, NE)	W 27 - 17	2-1
Fri 9/18	Nebraska City (Nebraska City, NE)	W 39 - 8	3-1
Fri 9/25	@ Mount Michael Benedictine (Elkhorn, NE)	W 55 - 13	4-1
Fri 10/2	@ Gross Catholic (Omaha, NE)	W 20 - 13	5-1
Fri 10/9	Crete (Crete, NE)	W 22 - 15	6-1
Fri 10/16	Norris (Firth, NE)	L 31 - 29	6-2
Fri 10/23	@ Pius X (Lincoln, NE)	L 31 - 18	6-3
Fri 10/30	@ McCook (McCook, NE) 2015 NSAA State Football Championships - Class B	L 14 - 8	6-4

ABOUT THE AUTHOR

Steve Banner spent most of his working career in adult education in the telecommunications industry before changing his path to tax and accounting, and then finally to his longed-for field of travel writing. He counts himself blessed to have two wonderful children and to be married to his very supportive and patient wife.